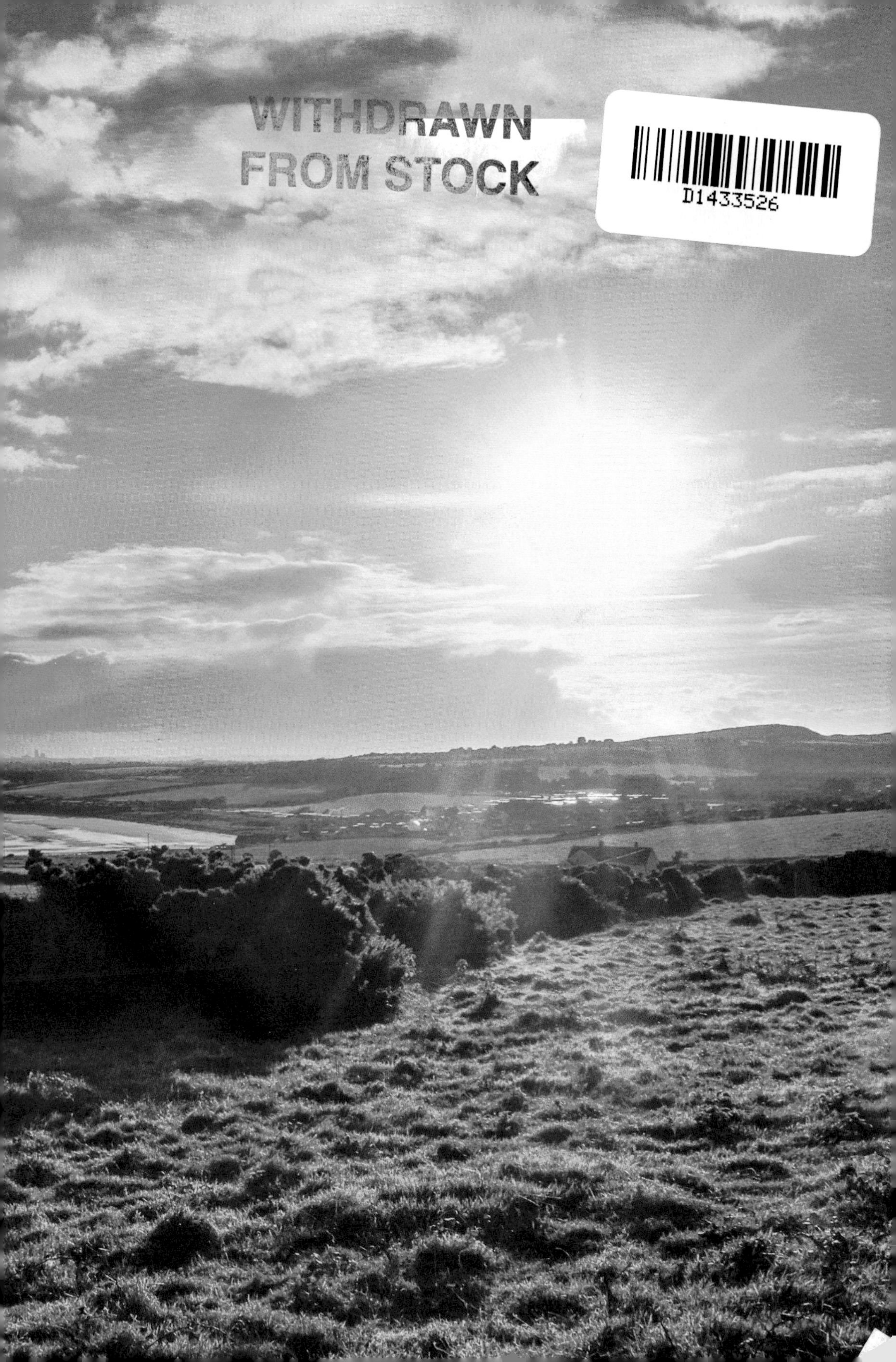

GOOD
FOOD
NO STRESS

GOOD
FOOD
NO STRESS

TARA WALKER

MERCIER PRESS
IRISH PUBLISHER – IRISH STORY

For Dad and Rob: to Dad for teaching me about food all my life, in spite of our lively debates, and to my love, Rob, for always encouraging and supporting me.

And for my late father-in-law, Alan, for his never-ending encouragement and infectious enthusiasm, and for putting pen to paper with all his ideas for 'The Tasty Tart'.

CONTENTS

CASUAL SUPPERS FOR FRIENDS

CATERING FOR A CROWD

SIDES

BARBECUE

SIDES

DESSERT

STRESS-FREE SUNDAY ROASTS

SIDES

MEAL-IN-A-BOWL SUPER SOUPS

COOKING WITH KIDS

I WOULD LIKE TO THANK THE FOLLOWING PEOPLE FOR THEIR HELP AND SUPPORT:

Sonia Sima, the stalwart of the East Coast Cookery School, who has been at my side since the beginning through both thick and thin and who calmly keeps the show on the road.

All the lovely people who have attended my cookery classes over the last few years and have given me the opportunity to do what I love doing most – cooking and talking about food. Also all the kids and parents of those kids who have attended our cookery camp, one of my favourite parts of everything we do at the cookery school.

Patricia Byrne, for her practical help and all the healthy muffins! Martha McCabe, for her friendliness, cheerfulness and efficiency.

Sinead Meegan, who typed the edits with me and kept me focused and cheery through a hair-pulling exercise!

My very good Cordon Bleu friend and kindred spirit Paula Kane, for helping me realise my vision for this book.

Laura Santtini, for allowing the use of the Flash Matcha + Ma-Yo Crusted Salmon with Flash Aglio Olio Peperoncino Brown Rice.

Kristin Jensen, who guided me through the early stages of this book, and all at Mercier Press, especially Mary Feehan, for giving me the opportunity to publish this book after our brief encounter at the airport, and Wendy Logue for making sense of my sometimes non-exact recipes and vagueries – writing this book has been a learning curve!

Photographer Rob Kerkvliet and food stylist Jette Virdi, who did such a wonderful job with the pictures.

My lovely friend Liz Farrell, who chats to me endlessly about food and who has the warmest home and hugs.

Finally I want to give particular thanks to the local community around beautiful Termonfeckin who have supported my little local business, and to all our local suppliers around Termonfeckin and Drogheda: Gareth's Family Butchers, Kirwan's Fish Cart, Tuites Butchers, Forge Field Farm Shop, Quintessential Wines and Drummond House Garlic.

'COOKING AND CRAIC'

ABOUT ME

Food has always been in my blood. Throughout my life my parents have had food businesses of one sort or another and it was my dad who first taught me to cook. My memories of my school-going days all involve going to Branagans, the restaurant they owned for eighteen years, after school and doing my homework. As soon as it was done satisfactorily, I could go to the chef in the kitchen and order my tea. My favourite had to be chicken Kiev with sautéed potatoes and an extra portion of garlic butter. While I was eating, the waitresses would be busily preparing the restaurant for the evening rush. I loved watching to see what would be written on the specials' board and how the candles, music, dimmed light and reserved signs could give the room a welcoming and enticing atmosphere. Then, before the first diners arrived, I would be sent home.

When I reached the age of fifteen, I was given the chance to work as a waitress. I loved the buzz and energy of it all, and found the banter, craic and happy, satisfied customers addictive. Although it was hard work, the wages and tips made up for the sore feet and tired legs. Also, having a little bit of independence was so satisfying at that age. There were downsides too, of course. Where we lived was just a three-minute walk from the restaurant, and it seemed that every time I was just about to watch a video the phone would ring and I would have to help out and hop 'onto starters' or do the dreaded wash-up! Still, that bar and restaurant was the centre of our family's world for eighteen years and although other businesses came and went, it is the one that looms largest in my childhood memories.

As time went on, I found myself wanting to work more and more in the kitchen and I finally got my chance one summer when I was nineteen. My parents had taken over a restaurant in a local golf club and I ran the kitchen during the week. I loved it. From ordering and prepping to cooking, I revelled in the variety of the days. There was never a dull moment. I loved how cooking consumed every part of my mind and body, and how suddenly five hours could have passed without me even noticing.

At this point, I should mention that during term time I was studying business and politics at Trinity College Dublin. I loved the social life and being at Trinity, but the subject matter was not for me and sitting still for long periods to study was excruciating. I am smiling to myself as I write this, because it is the very reason it has taken me so long to write this book! As I sit here trying to concentrate, I have to pull my mind away from the pineapple sitting on the counter beside me and all the wonderful things I could do with it.

As soon as I finished college I took a job as assistant manager in a start-up restaurant in Dublin. However, the kitchen was still where I wanted to be and the highlight of my day was talking to our head chef, Georg (still a good friend), about the evening's specials. Soon after this, a food-based trip to Venice and a stint in a restaurant in Edinburgh affirmed my desire to work in, rather than outside, the kitchen. Then, just as I was doing more and more research into food, my father became ill and I was drawn back home and into the family business again.

Life and the restaurant were busy and it was there I stayed for the best part of my twenties. I learned a lot about the running of a food business — controlling costs, dealing with regulations, staff, finance, and so on — but, more and more, I wanted to experiment in the kitchen. A four-day course in Ballymaloe sealed the deal for me in terms of what I wanted to do. I loved the variety of dishes, the respect for the land and seasonality, the whole ethos. Having seen this passion, I knew this was what I wanted for my future.

So, in 2008 I decided to make a big change and left the family business. I enrolled at Le Cordon Bleu in Paris and packed my bags. I stayed for three months and did an intensive version of the course. This meant long days, six days a week, but it was a fantastic experience. The environment of a cookery school is one I love — all the new recipes, the constant conversation about food, the camaraderie of it makes it a very nice place to be. The most intense memory I have of that time is the market that took place every second day in the area. The older ladies would bring wheelie trolleys and almost run you over in a bid to get the best produce. The market was huge, with farmers and sellers from the surrounding countryside coming into the city early in the morning to sell their produce.

At first, it irked me that I couldn't buy chillies or coriander or feta cheese (staples in my kitchen), but soon I realised that by buying what is produced locally and in season, I got the freshest and tastiest produce. No nasty, hard cherry tomatoes here. Instead of going to a big chain supermarket once a

week, where everything is mass-produced and has often travelled around the world, the locals were only buying enough food to cater for the next couple of meals. I'm not saying there aren't people in France who do a weekly shop in a supermarket, but I noticed that many people who lived in Paris didn't. It probably helps that most Parisians have very small kitchens, so this way of shopping just worked for them.

On my return to Ireland, I did a stage at the Chapter One restaurant. This was a great learning experience for me and cemented my desire to share my newfound know-ledge. Soon after this, I began working as a cookery tutor at Fairyhouse Cookery School and at the ICA's learning headquarters, An Grianán in Termonfeckin. In the following months, after some requests, I started to hold cookery-demonstration evenings at my own home under the name 'The Tasty Tart'. My aim was to create the lovely atmosphere of a restaurant and a sense of occasion, com-bined with a useful class filled with lots of tips to help people in the kitchen. I wanted to teach people how to make really good food but in a non-pretentious and welcoming way, with a bit of fun thrown in (our motto was 'Cooking and Craic').

In December 2010 and January 2011 I went to London to be the home economist and recipe tester on Laura Santtini's cookbook called *Flash Cooking*. The book focused on different parts of the world and on healthy eating. I tested every single recipe in the book meticulously, as well as lots of recipes that didn't make the final cut. That experience has probably been the biggest influence on my cooking style to date. Fresh, healthy and tasty, with a local and seasonal twist, is the best way to describe my cooking.

Back home, I was soon very busy with cookery classes and expecting my first child. The house I lived in with my husband was just too small for a baby and constant cookery classes, so we built a house just outside Termonfeckin and purpose built the kitchen for cookery classes. I am pleased to say that what is now the East Coast Cookery School has been a great success. I still have a great passion for food and for teaching, and I hope this book reflects my belief that the kitchen is the true heart of the home.

ABOUT THE BOOK

The aim of this book is to help take the stress out of cooking. As a busy mum and owner of a business, I understand the need for tasty and nutritious meals that relieve stress as opposed to adding to it. So the recipes in this book are easy to follow and don't involve any tricky techniques or culinary skills. They are also about making the most of what you have in your store cupboard and freezer, so you don't have to go shopping for dinner every day. You can use the days when you have a little spare time to prepare for the days you are under pressure.

During my cooking lessons, a common issue that people raise is lack of knowledge on what combinations of ingredients work well. Personally, I relish the idea of looking in a fairly empty fridge and conjuring up a tasty and nutritious meal with what's in my store cupboard and freezer. This book will help you to make the most of the food you do have and save you from having to rush off to the shop every evening, or worse, dial the take-away. Moreover, if you can use what you have, it will potentially cut down your weekly food bill and could help with the growing issue of food waste. It is my hope that this book will help you become more 'efficient' cooks, whilst not compromising on flavour or nutrition.

The recipes range from fast, easy meals to longer, more time-consuming dishes, which are suitable for entertaining. Many of the recipes have a handy hint or tip accompanying them. I've also put in a planner to show you how to use leftovers or a primary recipe to make up to four meals, which should help with those days of the week when you don't have the time or energy to cook. For example, if you roast a chicken on Sunday, you can use it to make a quick chicken and mushroom pie or Vietnamese spring rolls on Monday, then use the last small bits of meat from the carcass to make a Thai chicken noodle broth on Tuesday. I've also added a table with suggested combinations for lunch.

There's also a chapter on cooking with kids. I felt I just had to include this chapter because I run lots of kids' cookery camps at the school and we get great feedback from the parents, many of whom tell me that their children are now eating foods they would previously have shunned. It can be very stressful when you have gone to the trouble of making a healthy and well-balanced meal only to have your child push it away. I am a firm believer in getting the kids involved, as it usually gives them a better appreciation of the food itself and of the effort that goes in to preparing a meal. One thing that many parents have mentioned to me is the mess that is made by kids in the kitchen, but if you don't give them a chance, they'll never learn. And you never know ... I've had quite a few parents text me to tell me they are sipping a glass of wine while their children make dinner!

As you go through the recipes in this book you will probably notice my love of Middle and Far Eastern flavours. This is not because of any great adventures I have had in those parts of the world, but more due to my love for great flavours that are healthy and wholesome. Having trained at Le Cordon Bleu I also have a great appreciation for the classic techniques and flavours of French gastronomy, but on a day-to-day basis the most important thing for me is to eat food that is fresh, full of flavour, nutritious and energy boosting. Traditional French-based cuisine is fantastic at the weekend and on special occasions but, as I am a busy, self-employed mum, food has to fuel me and I don't want to feel heavy the next morning.

I recommend making everything from scratch so that you are not eating any nasty, hidden ingredients unknowingly. Shop-bought curry pastes, pestos, sauces and dressings often contain lots of sugar and salt, not to mention chemical preservatives. It is quick and easy to make these from scratch when you have a well-stocked cupboard. From my own experience living in the countryside with a small child, going to the shops is a hassle and it is usually easier to make my own than to contend with getting a small child in and out of a car seat!

It is my hope that this book will inspire you to experiment with new flavours and techniques and stop you reaching for convenience foods. I hope you enjoy cooking the recipes as much as I do.

Tara

PLANNING AHEAD

Here are some ideas for items that can be made at the weekend or on days
when you have more time, which can then be used on the following days
for other recipes, so you can have good food without the stress every day!

MAKE THE ROAST CHICKEN AND ROAST POTATOES ON PAGES 194 AND 201 AND USE THE LEFTOVERS FOR:

Thai Noodle Broth   Quesadillas

Vietnamese Spring Rolls   Potato Hash

MAKE THE PIZZA DOUGH ON PAGE 112 AND FREEZE IN PORTIONS TO USE FOR:

Bread Rolls

Tear'n'Share Bread

Naan Breads (just griddle like you would a normal naan, see p. 165)

MAKE THE TOMATO SAUCE ON PAGE 222 TO USE FOR:

Homemade Baked Beans   Chicken Parmigiana

Pizza   Prawn Arrabbiata

MAKE THE THAI CURRY PASTE ON PAGE 50 AND FREEZE INTO BATCHES FOR:

Curry   Butternut Squash Soup

Fish Cakes   Prawn and Sesame Stir Fry

MAKE THE SHORTBREAD ON PAGE 267 AND FREEZE INTO PORTIONS TO USE FOR:

Strawberries with Basil

Little Lemon Gems

Millionaire's Shortbread

MAKE THE SALTED CARAMEL ON PAGE 263 AND USE FOR:

Millionaire's Shortbread

Mini Banoffee Pies

MAKE THE LEMON CURD ON PAGE 254 FOR:

Meringue Swirls

Little Lemon Gems

LOVELY LUNCHES

Lunch is an important part of a working day but often we put little thought into it. To keep yourself sharp in the afternoon and prevent that terrible 3 p.m. slump, it is better to try to get a good mix of vegetables, proteins and slow-release carbohydrates than to choose the easy option of a ham and cheese sandwich.

The table below is not a set of recipes, but provides a guideline of ingredients that go well together and can be used to create healthy and nutritious lunches. All of these combinations are great to bring in a lunch-box with the dressing separate, but also for picnics. This is the sort of lunch I love to eat on days when I have no classes but a lot of admin to get through and I want to eat 'al desko'.

GRAIN/PULSE	PROTEIN	VEGETABLES	HERBS	DRESSING	NUTS/SEEDS
Quinoa	Hot smoked salmon	Cucumber, cherry tomatoes and avocado	Flat-leaf parsley	Lemon and extra virgin olive oil	Pumpkin and sunflower seeds
Spelt	Hard-boiled egg	Asparagus and red pepper	Flat-leaf parsley	Apple cider vinegar and rapeseed oil	Toasted flaked almonds
Lentils	Goat's cheese	Tomato, red onion and baby spinach leaves	Basil	Sherry vinegar and walnut oil	Candied walnuts

GRAIN/PULSE	PROTEIN	VEGETABLES	HERBS	DRESSING	NUTS/SEEDS
Pearl barley	Smoked mackerel	Little Gem leaves and blanched broccoli	Chives	Lemon and extra virgin olive oil	Pecan nuts
Bulgur	Feta	Olives, radishes and orange segments	Mint	Orange juice and harissa	Toasted pistachios
Cannellini beans	Tuna	Avocado, blanched green beans and chicory	Coriander	Lemon and extra virgin olive oil	Hazelnuts
Chickpeas	Chicken	Rocket leaves and roasted beetroot		Lemon tahini	Toasted sesame seeds
	Feta	Roast butternut squash, seasoned with herbes de Provence, sea salt and pepper	Rocket	Roasted pumpkin seed oil	Toasted pumpkin seeds
Mixed beans: chickpea, kidney and pinto		Avocado, tomato, sweetcorn, red and yellow pepper, and spring onion	Coriander	Lime, extra virgin olive oil	

STORE CUPBOARD ESSENTIALS

A NOTE ON OILS: I like to have a few different oils in my store cupboard but to keep things simple if you don't have the space or the inclination, use rapeseed oil for cooking at high temperatures and a bog standard olive oil (not extra virgin) for cooking at lower temperatures. You can also use sunflower, groundnut or vegetable oil for cooking at high temperatures. For drizzling or dressings use the best quality extra virgin olive oil you can afford. Sesame oil burns at low temperatures so it's always better to add it at the end of cooking for its flavour.

A NOTE ON SALTS: I usually keep two types of salt. I use a local fine sea salt called Oriel sea salt for cooking with and good-quality sea salt flakes such as Maldon or Atlantic sea salt for seasoning at the end of a dish when it won't be cooked any further.

A NOTE ON YOGHURT: Greek yoghurt is a fantastic ingredient to keep in the fridge: it has a high protein content and is naturally low in fat. It's a great base for lots of flavours, both savoury and sweet, and you can use it to whip up a quick, tasty sauce, such as the raita on page 58, the lime yoghurt on page 125, or the Indian-style dip on page 98. The Matcha topping on page 75 also makes a lovely dip. These are perfect for a quick, tasty accompaniment to grilled or baked meat, fish and vegetables.

IN THE FRIDGE

Jar of roasted peppers
Mozzarella
Sweet chilli sauce
Parmesan cheese
Chorizo
Butter
Feta
Crème fraîche
Tahini
Harissa paste
Tomato purée
Goat's cheese
Mayonnaise
Ketchup
Greek yoghurt
Eggs
Redcurrant jelly
Streaky bacon
Fresh chillies
Oyster sauce

FOR THE FREEZER

Bacon lardons
Wholemeal pittas
Wholemeal wraps
Peas
Prawns
Frozen mixed berries
Puff pastry
Part-baked baguettes or ciabattas
Round steak mince

NUTS + SEEDS

Pine nuts
Unsalted cashew nuts
Pistachio nuts
Unsalted peanuts
Flaked almonds
Walnuts
Hazelnuts
Pumpkin seeds
Sunflower seeds
Sesame seeds (black and white)
Poppy seeds

SPICES

Cumin, whole and ground
Coriander, whole and ground
Peppercorns
Chilli, flakes and powder
Cinnamon, sticks and powder
Cardamom, pods and ground
Cloves, whole and ground
Star anise
Ground ginger
Turmeric
Mixed spice
Allspice
Saffron strands
Paprika, sweet and smoked
Mixed herbs
Nutmeg
Cayenne pepper
Sea salt flakes

Ground sea salt
Mustard powder
Bay leaves
Fennel seeds
Vanilla extract, paste and pods
Cloves
Garam Masala
Herbes de Provence
Powdered stock or stock cubes (chicken, beef, vegetable, lamb and fish)
Mustard, wholegrain
Ras el hanout
Caraway seeds
Fenugreek
Chinese five spice

SAUCES

Soy sauce
Nam pla
Worcestershire sauce
Tabasco

VINEGARS

Rice wine vinegar
White wine vinegar
Cider vinegar
Red wine vinegar
Balsamic vinegar

OILS

Rapeseed oil
Olive oil, standard and extra virgin
Toasted sesame oil

SWEET THINGS

Honey

Cocoa powder

Golden syrup

Maple syrup

DRY INGREDIENTS

Baking powder

Bicarbonate of soda

Plain flour

Self-raising flour

Wholemeal flour,
extra coarse and fine ground

Cornflour

Dried yeast sachets

Ground almonds

Noodles

Pasta

Cream of tartare

Desiccated coconut

Caster sugar

Soft light-brown sugar

Icing sugar

Porridge oats

Dark, milk and white chocolate

Digestive biscuits

Peas

GRAINS

Couscous

Bulgur wheat

Basmati rice

Red split lentils

Rice paper

Arborio rice

DRIED FRUITS

Apricots

Sultanas

Currants

Cranberries

Dates

Crystallised ginger

CANNED GOODS

Tinned tomatoes

Chickpeas

Sweetcorn

Tuna

Mixed beans

Coconut milk

Cannellini beans

Green lentils

BRUNCH

· · · · · · · · · · · · · · · · · · · ·

SUNDAY MORNINGS ARE MY FAVOURITE TIME OF THE WEEK. I GIVE COOKERY CLASSES ON FRIDAY NIGHTS AND ALL DAY SATURDAY, SO AM GLAD OF A REST. WITH THIS IN MIND, I WANT TO DO AS LITTLE WORK IN THE KITCHEN AS POSSIBLE, WHILE STILL HAVING A DELICIOUS AND RESTORATIVE BRUNCH. YOU'LL SEE THAT I LOVE SERVING TABASCO WITH MANY OF MY EGG RECIPES, AS I LOVE THE CHILLI KICK TO WAKE ME UP, BUT THIS IS JUST A PERSONAL PREFERENCE.

HUEVOS RANCHEROS

SERVES 2-4

(DEPENDING ON HOW HUNGRY YOU ARE)

My favourite brunch dish by far! Traditionally, the sauce should be spicy, but as my daughter suddenly went off spicy food, I now add some Tabasco to my eggs at the table. If this is not an issue for you, add a teaspoon of dried chilli flakes with the garlic. On a separate note, many people swear by this as a hangover cure, not that I would know anything about that!

• • • • • • • • • • • • • •

1 teaspoon rapeseed oil

1 red onion, chopped

A pinch of sea salt

1 red pepper, sliced

1 clove of garlic, roughly chopped

1 teaspoon dried chilli flakes (optional)

1 x 400g tin of chopped tomatoes

4 eggs

Fresh coriander leaves

Place the oil in a large pan over a moderate heat, add the onion with a small pinch of salt and gently soften. When the onion has turned translucent, add the pepper and cook for a further minute, or until starting to soften. Add the garlic and chilli (if using) and cook for another 2 minutes.

Add the tin of tomatoes and allow to simmer on a gentle heat for at least 5 minutes to mature the sauce. In the meantime switch the grill on to a high heat.

When the sauce is cooked, make four wells in it and break the eggs into them. Keep simmering the sauce over a gentle heat until the egg whites have solidified.

Pop the whole pan under the grill for a minute or so until the egg yolks are cooked on the top but soft in the centre. Garnish with plenty of fresh coriander and serve. This goes really well with the potato and chorizo hash (see p. 33) or the avocado toast (see p. 31).

AVOCADO TOAST WITH POACHED EGGS

This might not be considered a recipe, but it's a great start to the day nonetheless and so definitely worth including. More importantly, it includes my technique for making the perfect poached egg!

SERVES 2

4 eggs

4 slices of low GI or multigrain bread, toasted

1 ripe avocado

Juice of ½ lime

Sea salt

Some fresh red chilli, chopped, or Tabasco sauce (optional)

Heat a fairly deep pot of water until it is just simmering. Break the eggs into little bowls or cups to give them shape, then gently slide the eggs into the pot.

Leave the eggs to cook for about 5 minutes or until the white has solidified and the yolk is still runny.

In the meantime, toast the bread and cut the avocado in half, pop out the stone and scoop the flesh out. Season the flesh of the avocado with the lime juice and some sea salt flakes. Mash with a fork and spread on the toast. I find the quickest and easiest way to mash avocado is on a chopping board.

Fold two pieces of kitchen roll in half and place one on your worktop. Using a large slotted spoon, remove the eggs carefully from the pot and place them on the kitchen roll. Gently place the other piece of kitchen roll on top of the eggs to dry them. This step is optional, but I find it essential as I hate having excess water all over my plate or avocado toast.

Carefully peel off the top layer of kitchen roll and slide the eggs back onto the slotted spoon one at a time. Place one on top of each slice of avocado toast. Top with the chilli or Tabasco sauce if using.

POTATO + CHORIZO HASH

SERVES 2-4

(DEPENDING ON HOW HUNGRY YOU ARE)

I usually make this with the huevos rancheros but it can also be a great brunch on its own. If you are having this with the huevos rancheros then you don't need the eggs, if you are having it on its own then it's one egg per person. This is a great way of using up leftover ham or veggies such as Brussels sprouts at Christmas, or cabbage and kale.

• • • • • • • • • • • • • • •

75g chorizo, chopped into small pieces

1 small onion, diced

Leftover potatoes (the equivalent of at least 2 potatoes)

2–4 eggs (optional)

1 teaspoon rapeseed or groundnut oil (optional)

1 spring onion, sliced

Fry the chorizo in a dry, non-stick pan for a minute or two until it releases its oil. Add the onion and sauté for another 2 minutes.

Add the leftover potatoes. Stir until crisp and golden.

Add the eggs (if using). If the pan is dry add a teaspoon of oil first, then move the potatoes and onion to the sides of the pan and break the eggs into the middle. Fry the eggs until they are cooked to your taste.

Serve immediately, garnishing with the spring onion.

INDIAN—STYLE LEFTOVER RICE + EGGS WITH BAKED MUSHROOMS

SERVES 2

This recipe actually came about one Sunday morning when I was in the midst of writing this book. Whilst doing a 'fridge forage' I discovered I had lots of rice leftover from the night before. This was the recipe I came up with to use it up and it got a big thumbs up from my family.

• • • • • • • • • • • • •

4 flat-cap mushrooms

A small knob of butter

1 tablespoon rapeseed oil

½ red onion, chopped

A pinch of salt

½ red pepper, finely chopped

A handful of cherry tomatoes, halved

½ teaspoon ground cumin

½ teaspoon ground coriander

½ teaspoon turmeric

150g leftover cooked rice

2 eggs

Jalapeño peppers (from a jar)

A handful of flat-leaf parsley, chopped

1 spring onion, finely chopped

Preheat the oven to 200°C/fan 180°C/gas mark 6.

Place the mushrooms in an ovenproof dish with the stalk facing upwards and dot each one with a little butter. Bake for 10–15 minutes.

When the mushrooms are nearly cooked, heat the oil in a large frying pan. Add the red onion and a pinch of salt and cook for 2–3 minutes.

Add the red pepper and cherry tomato halves to the frying pan, then add the cumin, coriander and turmeric and stir in the leftover rice.

When everything is coated nicely in the spices, make a couple of wells in the centre of the rice and break the eggs into them.

Cook until the eggs are set to your taste. You can pop the whole pan under the grill to ensure the top of the eggs are cooked.

Serve the rice and eggs garnished with jalapeños to taste, flat-leaf parsley and the spring onion, and two of the baked mushrooms each.

CINNAMON + GINGER FRENCH TOAST WITH MIXED-BERRY COMPOTE + MAPLE SYRUP

SERVES 2

French toast always seems to be a winner with young and old alike.

• • • • • • • • • • • • • • •

FOR THE TOAST:

1 egg

½ teaspoon cinnamon

½ teaspoon vanilla paste or extract

2 tablespoons milk

4 slices of white bread

A small knob of butter

A thumb-sized piece of fresh ginger, grated

Maple syrup to drizzle

FOR THE COMPOTE:

200g raspberries, blackberries, loganberries or tayberries

2–4 tablespoons icing sugar

Put the ingredients for the compote in a saucepan and simmer gently for 10 minutes. Stir lightly so as not to break up the berries while simmering. Take off the heat and allow to cool.

While the compote is cooling, mix the egg, cinnamon, vanilla paste/extract and milk in a bowl until well combined. Dip the bread into the mixture, then leave it on a plate to allow the mixture to soak in.

Heat a frying pan and add the butter. When it's foaming, add the bread. Fry until golden brown and crisp on both sides. Remove to a plate, sprinkle with the ginger and drizzle with the maple syrup and the compote.

TARA'S TIP:

THE MIXED-BERRY COMPOTE IS ALSO GREAT OVER PANCAKES OR ICE CREAM. FROZEN BERRIES ARE USEFUL IN THE WINTER FOR THIS RECIPE.

CHURROS WITH HOT CHOCOLATE SAUCE

We made this at our very first kids' cookery camp and I still meet some of those children who say it was their favourite recipe. But it's not just for kids!

• • • • • • • • • • • • •

60g self-raising flour

60g plain flour

A pinch of salt

1 tablespoon olive oil

225g boiling water

2 teaspoons caster sugar

1 teaspoon cinnamon

50g dark chocolate

25g milk chocolate

1 teaspoon golden syrup

75g cream

Sunflower oil to fry

Place the flours and salt in a bowl and stir in the olive oil and water until the mixture forms a fairly tight dough. Leave to rest for a few minutes.

Mix the sugar and cinnamon together, place into a bowl big enough to dip the churros into and set aside.

In a pot, melt the chocolates and golden syrup into the cream, stirring until thick. Place in a bowl big enough to dip the churros into and keep warm until ready to serve.

Place the churros dough into a piping bag, then heat your sunflower oil to 190°C. You can either use a deep-fat fryer, which will have a temperature-control dial, or a deep frying pan with oil that is at least an inch deep in it. If you are using a frying pan, you can check the oil is hot enough by placing a teaspoon of the mixture into the oil. If it solidifies straight away, you are good to go!

Pipe approximately 5cm sections of the dough into the oil and cook for about 2 minutes on each side, turning occasionally to get an even golden-brown colour.

Dust with the cinnamon sugar and dip into the chocolate sauce, then enjoy.

THIN + CRISPY OLD-FASHIONED PANCAKES

MAKES 10

My husband and I always have the same disagreement over thin and crispy or thick and fluffy pancakes; he prefers the thin and crispy and I like the thick and fluffy. When it comes to savoury fillings, though, it has to be thin and crispy!

• • • • • • • • • • • • • • • • •

2 tablespoons plain flour

¼ pint milk

1 egg

1 teaspoon butter, melted

Salt and pepper to taste

Rapeseed oil for frying

Mix together all the ingredients except the oil and leave to rest for up to 2 hours.

Heat a teaspoon of oil in a frying pan. Add a small ladleful of batter to the middle of the pan and tilt the pan in circles until the batter has spread into a nice thin layer.

Flip or turn with a fish slice to cook both sides. Repeat this with the rest of the batter and add more oil as necessary.

Make the pancakes ahead of time and leave on a plate over a pot of boiling water covered with another plate to keep warm while you prepare your filling. This can be whatever you like, but what follows are some of my favourites.

PANCAKE FILLINGS
SMOKED SALMON,
CREAM CHEESE + CHIVES

Pancakes with this filling are delicious rolled up, sliced and served as canapés.

Cream cheese

Smoked salmon, sliced into thin ribbons

A handful of chives, thinly sliced

Juice of ½ lemon

Black pepper

Spread some cream cheese thinly across each pancake and place a few thin slices of smoked salmon in the middle.

Sprinkle with the chives and squeeze a little lemon juice over the top.

Season with freshly ground black pepper.

Fold one edge of the pancake in, roll up and serve.

• ● • ● • ● • ● • ● • ● • ● • ● • ● • ● • ● • ● • ●

PANCAKE FILLINGS
ROAST RED PEPPER,
CHILLI + FETA CHEESE

1 jar of roasted red peppers (or homemade if you prefer), sliced

½ fresh red chilli, finely chopped (or more, according to how hot you like it)

150g feta cheese, crumbled or chopped

Salt and pepper

Place a couple of strips of the roasted red peppers on the pancake and sprinkle with the chilli (make sure you taste some of the chilli first so you know how hot it is!)

Place some of the feta cheese on top and season generously.

Fold one edge of the pancake in, roll up and serve.

PANCAKE FILLINGS
CHOCOLATE, HAZELNUT + BANANA

To make this slightly less sinful, use a couple of squares of good quality dark chocolate of at least 70% cocoa.

2 tablespoons chopped hazelnuts

Chocolate spread

Banana, sliced

Lightly toast the nuts on a dry frying pan.

Smooth the chocolate spread over the pancake and place banana slices down the middle. Top with the hazelnuts.

Fold one edge of the pancake in, roll up and serve.

• •

PANCAKE FILLINGS
TROPICAL FRUITS + CHOPPED NUTS

2 tablespoons chopped almonds or hazelnuts

1 teaspoon brown sugar per pancake

Your choice of tropical fruits such as mango, passion-fruit seeds or pineapple, chopped

Small tub of crème fraîche

Lightly toast the nuts on a dry frying pan.

Sprinkle the sugar over the pancake whilst it's still warm.

Place the fruit and nuts along the centre of the pancake and place a dollop of the crème fraîche on top.

Fold one edge of the pancake in, roll up and serve.

AMERICAN-STYLE BREAKFAST PANCAKES WITH BLUEBERRIES

MAKES 6

My favourite type of pancake, these are lovely and fluffy in the centre. Kids love making these in different shapes. To do so lightly oil some cookie cutters, place them into the frying pan, pour the batter into them and proceed as usual.

• • • • • • • • • • • • •

200g plain flour

1 teaspoon cream of tartar

½ teaspoon bicarbonate of soda

200ml milk

1 large egg

75g blueberries

1 teaspoon honey

Zest of 1 lemon

Butter, for cooking

SUGGESTED TOPPINGS:

Streaky bacon, cooked until crispy and chopped

Maple or birch syrup

Extra blueberries and/or raspberries

Mixed-berry compote (see p. 38)

A dollop of Greek yoghurt

Put the flour, cream of tartar and bicarbonate of soda into a large bowl. Mix well with a whisk.

Pour the milk into a large measuring jug. Break in the egg and mix well. Add the blueberries, honey and lemon zest and combine.

Pour some of the milk mixture into the flour mixture and mix well with a spatula. Keep adding the milk until you have used it all. You should get a smooth, thick pouring batter.

Heat a frying pan and coat with a little butter. Then spoon in the batter, 1 tablespoon for each pancake, in separate heaps. Bubbles will appear on top as the pancakes cook – turn them at this stage using a metal spatula. Cook until brown on the second side and keep warm on a plate, covered with foil. Repeat until all the mixture is used up.

Place whatever toppings you fancy on the pancakes and serve.

MONDAY NIGHT MEALS

· ·

OBVIOUSLY, THESE RECIPES DO NOT HAVE TO BE CONFINED
TO A MONDAY, BUT THE POINT OF THIS CHAPTER IS
TO PROVIDE YOU WITH RECIPES THAT WILL GIVE SOME
GOOD SUSTENANCE AT THE START OF THE WEEK YET
DON'T NEED ANY HARD WORK IN THE KITCHEN!

HEALTHY SALMON CHOW MEIN

SERVES 4

2 cloves of garlic, finely chopped

A thumb-sized piece of fresh ginger, grated

3 teaspoons tomato purée

2 tablespoons oyster sauce

2 tablespoons soy sauce

3 tablespoons cold water

2 nests of medium egg noodles

1 tablespoon rapeseed oil

2 salmon darne fillets, sliced into 3 lengthways

1 large red pepper, sliced

A large handful of mangetout, washed

A large handful of beansprouts, washed

2 spring onions, sliced

Juice of 1 lime

A few fresh coriander leaves and toasted sesame seeds

TARA'S TIP:

THE EASIEST WAY TO SERVE NOODLES IS TO USE TONGS.

A tasty, nutritious and fast dish that is a firm favourite in our family, especially with my four-year-old daughter.

• • • • • • • • • • • • •

To make the sauce, put the garlic and ginger in a bowl, add the tomato purée, oyster sauce, soy sauce and cold water and stir. Set aside.

Boil a large pan of water on the hob. When the water is boiling, drop in the noodles, turn off the heat and allow to sit for 5 minutes. Drain in a colander or a large sieve in the sink.

With everything prepared, you can now start cooking. Heat a wok over a high heat – it's hot enough when it starts to smoke. Add the oil and lay the slices of salmon on the wok carefully, ensuring all the pieces are in contact with the pan. After a minute or so, use a spatula to gently move the salmon around the wok until it is half cooked.

Add the pepper and mangetout and stir-fry for 1 minute. Then add the sauce and cook until it starts to bubble.

Add the noodles, beansprouts and spring onions, and toss in the sauce until they are well coated. Continue to cook, stirring constantly, until the beansprouts wilt a little.

Add the lime juice and check for taste. Add a little extra soy sauce if more seasoning is needed, or a few tablespoons of water if it's a little dry.

Serve in bowls, garnished with the coriander and sesame seeds.

PUMPKIN + MUSHROOM RISOTTO

I always say to people at my classes that risotto is a dish that can be therapeutic, as it forces you to slow down and chill out. If you're feeling impatient don't make it! You can use butternut squash if you can't find pumpkin.

• • • • • • • • • • • • •

200g pumpkin, peeled, deseeded and diced

Olive oil

2 sprigs of thyme, leaves removed

Salt and pepper

1 teaspoon butter

1 onion, finely chopped

100g mushrooms, chopped

1 clove of garlic, finely chopped

200g Arborio risotto rice

750ml chicken or vegetable stock

½ lemon

100g Parmesan, grated

2 sprigs of flat-leaf parsley, finely chopped

Preheat the oven to 200°C/fan 180°C/gas mark 6.

Put the pumpkin into a roasting dish with a little oil. Toss the pumpkin in the oil with a few of the thyme leaves and season to taste. Roast for 20–30 minutes or until softened.

Put some olive oil and the butter into a pan over a medium heat and gently sweat your onion with a little salt until softened. When the onion is almost ready, add the mushrooms, garlic and the remaining thyme leaves and stir for a couple of minutes.

Add the rice to the pan, stirring to make sure the rice is coated in the butter and oil. If necessary, add a little more butter.

Now, start to add the stock, a ladleful at a time, stirring all the time. Add each new ladleful when the one before is fully absorbed. It should take 20–25 minutes for all the liquid to be absorbed.

To finish, add the pumpkin and a squeeze of fresh lemon juice, stir the Parmesan cheese through and serve topped with the parsley.

PRAWN + SESAME STIR-FRY

SERVES 4

Although I am including the recipe for the Thai curry paste here, you should make up a large batch of this when you have time and then you can freeze it in small batches and just use a couple of teaspoons when you are making this stir-fry.

• • • • • • • • • • • •

FOR THE THAI CURRY PASTE:

2 teaspoons coriander seeds

2 teaspoons cumin seeds

2 fresh red chillies, chopped coarsely

1 green chilli, chopped coarsely

2 large cloves of garlic

2 onions, chopped roughly

2 sticks of fresh lemongrass

3 kaffir lime leaves

Zest of ½ lime

1 teaspoon finely chopped ginger

½ cup fresh coriander, stalks and leaves

1 teaspoon shrimp paste

A pinch of chilli flakes

1 tablespoon peanut oil

2 tablespoons soy sauce

1 tablespoon nam pla (Thai fish sauce)

FOR THE SAUCE:

2 tablespoons oyster or hoisin sauce

1 tablespoon fish sauce

2 tablespoons soy sauce

2 tablespoons sesame oil

2 tablespoons lime juice

First make the curry paste. Heat the coriander and cumin seeds in a pan until fragrant. Place in a pestle and mortar and grind to a fine powder.

Place the powder and the rest of the ingredients, excluding the oil and sauces, in a food processor and blitz until it forms a smooth paste. Stop and scrape down the sides of the processor as you blitz to make sure everything is properly blended.

Add the peanut oil, soy sauce and nam pla and combine.

For the stir-fry, mix all the sauce ingredients together and set aside.

Heat a large non-stick frying pan or wok over high heat for 5 minutes. Add the sesame seeds to the pan, dry roast for a few minutes until browned, remove and set aside.

Cook the noodles according to the pack instructions.

Add 1 tablespoon of the oil to a pan or wok and swirl around to coat the base and sides. Make sure it is very hot. You should only be able to keep your hand over it for a second or so.

FOR THE STIR-FRY:

1 tablespoon sesame seeds

4 portions of egg noodles

3 tablespoons groundnut oil

200g mangetout, baby corn and pepper, cut to similar-sized pieces

200g beansprouts

2 large handfuls of prawns or langoustines, shelled

A handful of coriander, chopped

1 red chilli, deseeded and finely chopped

Add 2 teaspoons of the curry paste and then add the vegetables, starting with the one that takes longest to cook. If using the ingredients listed here, baby corn takes the longest, next the peppers, then the mangetout and finally the beansprouts. Stir-fry for a few minutes until slightly cooked but still firm.

Add the prawns to the wok and stir-fry for another minute.

Add in the sauce and stir-fry for another minute.

Add the noodles to the wok and mix well.

Garnish with chopped coriander, chilli and toasted sesame seeds.

TARA'S TIP:

YOU CAN USE CHICKEN IF YOU DON'T LIKE PRAWNS, IT TASTES JUST AS GOOD – JUST COOK IN YOUR HOT WOK UNTIL BROWNED, BEFORE ADDING THE CURRY PASTE. I HAVE LISTED THE VEGETABLES I LIKE TO STIR-FRY, BUT THESE CAN BE CHANGED TO WHATEVER YOU LIKE.

PRAWNS ARRABBIATA WITH SPELT SPAGHETTI

SERVES 2

One of my go-to Monday night meals, this is light, healthy and very fast.

• • • • • • • • • • • • •

2 tablespoons olive oil

1 clove of garlic, crushed

Salt

A pinch of chilli flakes

1 x 400g tin of chopped tomatoes

1 teaspoon sugar

100g spelt spaghetti

Pepper

16 prawns (approx.), shelled
(I prefer to use Dublin Bay prawns)

30ml cream (optional)

Heat the oil in a wide, shallow saucepan and gently sauté the garlic with a pinch of salt until soft, and then add the chilli flakes. Stir in the tomatoes and sugar. Bring to a simmer and cook for 5–10 minutes.

Cook the pasta according to the instructions on the packet. You should time this to be ready at the same time as the sauce.

Season the sauce with salt and pepper to taste and add the prawns. If you are using the cream, add this at the same time.

Simmer until the prawns are just cooked through and, if using the cream, until the sauce thickens. You will know the prawns are cooked when they turn opaque – this should take no more than a couple of minutes.

Toss the pasta into the sauce in the pan and combine well to serve.

PAILLARD OF LEMON + ROSEMARY CHICKEN WITH A GREEN BEAN + PURPLE POTATO SALAD

SERVES 2

Bashing out the chicken fillet is a great way to cook it really fast and of course to release any frustrations you have. You can use any flavourings or side dishes with chicken cooked this way. This is my favourite version.

• • • • • • • • • • • • • • • •

2 chicken fillets

1 clove of garlic

Leaves from a couple of sprigs of rosemary

Zest of 1 lemon

A pinch of sea salt

Rapeseed oil

6 purple potatoes (or baby potatoes), cut into approx. 2cm chunks

100g green beans

FOR THE FRENCH DRESSING:

2 parts olive oil to 1 part white wine vinegar

1 teaspoon Dijon mustard

1 clove of garlic, peeled and bashed with the back of a knife

Salt and pepper

Place all the ingredients for the French dressing in a jar and shake well to combine. Set aside.

Place the chicken on a board and cover with cling film. Use a rolling pin to bash it until it is only about a ½cm thick.

In the meantime, in a pestle and mortar, grind the garlic, rosemary, lemon zest and sea salt together with just enough oil to make a paste. Rub half the paste over one side of the chicken. A silicone brush is handy for this, but make sure you don't dip the brush back into the marinade after touching the raw chicken. Leave to marinate for at least 30 minutes.

Place a pot of boiling, salted water on the hob on a high heat, add the potatoes and boil for 3 minutes, then add the green beans and boil for a further 2 minutes or until the potatoes are soft and the green beans are al dente. Drain.

Heat a frying pan until very hot and add a little rapeseed oil. Fry the chicken, marinade-side down, for about 2 minutes.

Turn the chicken over and spread the other half of the paste over the cooked side and leave to cook through. The idea is to use half the marinade initially and then flash-fry the remainder on the cooked side of the chicken to have a fresher finish.

While the chicken is cooking, toss the potatoes and green beans in the French dressing while still warm.

To serve, cut each chicken fillet into half-centimetre slices and place on top of the salad.

POTATO + SPINACH CURRY

SERVES 4

Groundnut oil

1 onion, finely chopped

A pinch of salt

1½ tablespoons tomato purée

350g potatoes, peeled and cubed

2 cloves of garlic, finely chopped

400ml vegetable stock

200g spinach leaves, washed

A handful of flaked almonds, toasted

A handful of coriander, chopped

FOR THE GOAN CURRY PASTE:

1 teaspoon cumin seeds

1 teaspoon coriander seeds

1 teaspoon black peppercorns

1 teaspoon fennel seeds

1 teaspoon turmeric

1 teaspoon sea salt

3 cloves of garlic

1 teaspoon tamarind paste

A thumb-sized piece of ginger, peeled

1 tablespoon red wine vinegar

1 teaspoon tomato purée

1 tablespoon groundnut oil

FOR THE RAITA (OPTIONAL):

100g Greek yoghurt

1 clove of garlic, minced or chopped finely

1 teaspoon lemon juice

1 sprig of fresh mint, finely chopped

½ cucumber

Salt and pepper

Even if you don't have all the ingredients for this curry paste, give it a go anyway, as any combination of spices with the 'blandish' potato will be delicious. If you can't be bothered making the raita, just use some natural or Greek yoghurt instead. This curry paste recipe makes approximately 5 tablespoons.

● ● ● ● ● ● ● ● ● ● ● ●

To make the curry paste, place the dry spices in a frying pan and toast gently, until fragrant and popping slightly. Transfer to a pestle and mortar and grind with the sea salt. Add the rest of the ingredients to a food processor and blitz with the dry spice mixture until you have a smooth paste.

Heat a heavy-based saucepan and add a glug of groundnut oil. Add the onion with a pinch of salt and sweat with a lid on for a few minutes until softened.

Add the curry paste and tomato purée and cook for a couple of minutes. Then add the potatoes, garlic and vegetable stock and simmer for about 10 minutes or until the potatoes have softened. Finally, add the spinach in for the final 2 minutes of cooking.

While the curry is cooking make the raita. Combine the yoghurt, garlic, lemon juice and mint. Cut the cucumber in half lengthways and remove the seeds with a teaspoon. Chop it finely and add it to the yoghurt. Season to taste.

Serve with some rice and topped with a dollop of raita, some toasted flaked almonds and the coriander.

LEMON, GARLIC + YOGHURT–MARINATED CHICKEN

SERVES 4

This simple chicken dish is also ideal for the barbecue. Simply thread the chicken onto skewers and cook in the same way. The metal skewers are helpful as they conduct the heat and help to cook the chicken from the inside out. I usually use one chicken breast for two people as the yoghurt coating bulks it out and makes it more substantial, but feel free to use one chicken breast per person.

• ● • ● • ● • ● • ● • ● • ●

2 tablespoons plain Greek yoghurt

Zest of 1 lemon

1 clove of garlic, minced

2 chicken breast fillets, sliced lengthways to give about 6 pieces per fillet

1 sprig of rosemary, leaves removed and finely chopped (optional)

Place the yoghurt, lemon zest and garlic in a bowl and add the chicken pieces and rosemary (if using). Refrigerate and allow to marinate for at least an hour.

Place on a medium heat on a hot griddle pan, turning every 3 minutes or so to ensure it is evenly cooked. You can check the very centre of one piece to be sure.

This is lovely served with a carpaccio of courgette salad (see p. 62), or, if you are barbecuing, with barbecued vegetables (see p. 182).

SIDES

CARPACCIO OF COURGETTE SALAD WITH MINT, CHILLI + PARMESAN

SERVES 4

This dish is really only worth making if you come across some lovely young courgettes at a farmer's market or similar, or of course if you grow your own. It must be prepared just before serving for the best results.

• • • • • • • • • • • • • •

8–10 young, in-season courgettes, sliced on a mandolin or very finely with a knife or food processor

1 red chilli, finely chopped

A handful of young mint leaves, torn

50g Parmesan cheese, shaved

Juice of ½ lemon

A glug of good quality extra virgin olive oil

Sea salt flakes

Place a layer of courgette slices on a plate with a little of the chilli, mint and Parmesan cheese. Drizzle a little lemon juice over this layer, then add some sea salt flakes and a drizzle of the oil. Repeat to build a nice layered salad.

HEALTHY, WHOLESOME + HASTY

· · · · · · · · · · · · · · · ·

THESE RECIPES ARE BASED ON A VERY POPULAR COOKERY CLASS THAT WE RUN AT THE SCHOOL, AND THAT CLASS, IN TURN, IS BASED ON A COOKBOOK I WORKED ON AS HOME ECONOMIST/RECIPE TESTER CALLED *FLASH COOKING* BY LAURA SANTTINI.

MY CLASS IS ALL ABOUT USING HERBS, SPICES AND ZESTS TO CREATE HIGH PROTEIN, LOW GI DISHES THAT ARE FILLING AND NUTRITIOUS FOR PEOPLE WHO ARE SHORT ON TIME BUT NEED LOTS OF ENERGY AND LOTS OF FLAVOUR.

ASIAN BEEF SALAD

SERVES 2

This is the ultimate healthy fast food. Choose a good well-aged piece of fillet steak. Ask your butcher to give you the longest-aged steak they have in stock. It is worth doing this as the dish really relies on the flavour of the beef. It is very important to rest the steak after cooking for at least 5 minutes to get a nice tender result. The beef in this recipe should be served rare to medium rare and sliced very thinly.

• • • • • • • • • • • •

400g lean beef steak
(sirloin or fillet)
Green salad leaves of your choice

FOR THE MARINADE:
2 cloves of garlic, minced
10ml rice wine vinegar
10ml Tamari soy sauce
10ml groundnut oil

FOR THE ORIENTAL DRESSING:
1 clove of garlic
1 teaspoon grated fresh ginger
2 tablespoons soy sauce
2 tablespoons honey
1 tablespoon rice wine vinegar
2 tablespoons olive oil
1 tablespoon sesame oil

Combine the marinade ingredients and marinate the beef in the fridge for 2 hours. Then remove from the fridge and allow to return to room temperature before cooking.

Heat a griddle pan until very hot. Place the steak on the griddle (no need for oil). Cook the steak the way you like it – I recommend medium rare for this dish, but it's up to you. Leave to rest in a warm place for a minimum of 5 minutes but preferably 10–15 minutes.

While the meat is resting, prepare the Oriental dressing by mixing all the ingredients in a bowl.

To serve, place some green salad leaves on a plate and top with slices of the marinated beef steak. Drizzle some dressing on top. You can also heat up the rest of the marinade and drizzle it over for extra flavour and warmth.

TARA'S TIP:
TO COOK A PIECE OF STEAK THAT'S ABOUT AN INCH THICK RARE TO MEDIUM RARE, COOK FOR 2–3 MINUTES ON EACH SIDE AT A VERY HIGH TEMPERATURE.

BRILL WITH CORIANDER, CHILLI + LEMON DRESSING

SERVES 2

This is another of my favourite midweek meals, and my husband and I have been having it for years as it is so quick and easy to make. You can use any flat white fish for this dish, but my favourites are John Dory, turbot and brill. Make the dressing first to let it infuse while you prepare the rest of the dish.

• ● • ● • ● • ● • ● • ●

A small bunch of coriander

1 clove of garlic

1 red chilli

Juice of 1 lemon

3 tablespoons olive oil

Salt and pepper

Plain flour (just enough to coat the fish)

2 fillets of brill

Butter (not too cold)

Chop the coriander, garlic and chilli and add to a bowl along with the lemon juice. Add the olive oil, and salt and pepper to taste. Leave to infuse while the fish is cooking.

Place the flour on a plate and season with salt and pepper.

Pat the fish dry with kitchen roll or a clean tea towel, and dip into the flour to coat. Then spread the butter on the side of the fish without skin as if you were buttering a piece of bread.

Heat a frying pan on the hob until very hot. Place the fish flesh-side down on the pan – it should sizzle. When the fish 'domes' (i.e. rises up in the centre), turn it and cook for a couple of minutes on the skin side.

Remove to a warm plate and drizzle with the coriander and chilli dressing.

Serve with oven-roasted potato wedges (see p. 72) and salad, or steamed green vegetables, such as asparagus or tenderstem broccoli.

WARM SPELT SALAD WITH BUTTERNUT SQUASH, SMOKED CHICKEN + TARRAGON

SERVES 2

Spelt wholegrains are high in protein and low in gluten. I have been buying my spelt berries direct from Dunany Flour for years, but happily they are now selling these in supermarkets too. Any leftovers from this dish are great in a lunchbox at work the next day.

• • • • • • • • • • • • •

100g whole spelt berries

½ butternut squash

Olive oil

75g smoked chicken breast, chopped into bite-size pieces

1 shallot, finely chopped

2 sprigs of fresh tarragon, roughly chopped

A handful of flat-leaf parsley, chopped

FOR THE DRESSING:

2 tablespoons olive oil

1 tablespoon lemon juice

Salt and pepper to taste

Boil the spelt in 600ml of water for about 1 hour or until soft, or follow the pack instructions.

Mix together the ingredients for the dressing and set aside.

Preheat the oven to 180˚C/fan 160˚C/gas mark 4.

Slice the butternut squash into wedges (no need to peel), discarding the seeds. Place on a baking tray and drizzle generously with olive oil. Place in the oven for 25–35 minutes or until softened. When cool enough, use a tablespoon to scoop the flesh from the skin (this may not be necessary if the skin is soft enough). Discard the skin.

Mix the butternut squash and chicken into the spelt, then mix in the shallot and the herbs. Add the dressing and mix again. Serve while still warm.

TARA'S TIP:

IF YOU WANT TO MAKE MORE DRESSING, THEN THE QUANTITIES SHOULD BE TWO PARTS OLIVE OIL TO ONE PART LEMON JUICE.

FISH PARCELS + OVEN-ROASTED POTATO WEDGES

SERVES 2

These parcels are a very quick and easy way to cook fish and there is no washing up!! Use any type of fish you like with any combination of flavours, or you can also use chicken fillet instead of the fish, thinned as per the instructions on page 56. I like to use cod or haddock for this recipe but you can use any white fish you prefer.

• • • • • • • • • • • •

FOR THE FISH:

2 x 150g fillets of cod/ haddock (skinned)

4 mushrooms, sliced

1 small onion, diced

1 pinch of herbes de Provence for each piece of fish

A splash of white wine

FOR THE WEDGES:

4 medium-sized rooster potatoes

Salt and pepper

3 tablespoons olive oil

Preheat the oven to 180°C/fan 160°C/gas mark 4.

Cut the potatoes into wedge-shaped pieces. Place on a baking tray, season and drizzle with the olive oil. Cook for 20–30 minutes until soft.

Cut out a rectangular piece of parchment or baking paper large enough to hold the fish and wrap it up. Place the fish in the centre and place the other ingredients you are using on top.

Wrap up tightly and ensure the steam cannot escape.

Place on a baking tray and put in oven for 15–20 minutes (this depends on the thickness of the fish you are using). Check the fish is cooked through before serving.

Serve the fish with all the juices, a portion of wedges and some vegetables of your choice.

OTHER SUGGESTIONS TO USE WITH THE FISH:
Half a red onion, eight cherry tomatoes, a pinch of dried oregano and 30g of crumbled feta.

A handful of spinach, a clove of garlic and a small drop of cream, for each piece of fish.

A pinch of cumin, a slice of lime and a clove of garlic, thinly sliced, for each piece of fish.

A teaspoon of harissa paste brushed over each piece of fish, served with a nice with a dollop of Greek yoghurt when cooked.

A slice of orange, a pinch of smoked paprika, a slice of roast red pepper and a couple of Kalamata olives, for each piece of fish.

PORK CHOP WITH LEMON, ROSEMARY + CANNELLINI BEANS

SERVES 2

This is a handy one-pan dinner for those days when you are tired or in a hurry. If you don't have an ovenproof pan, then you can use tinfoil to cover the plastic handle on your pan if it is only going to be in the oven for a few minutes.

• • • • • • • • • • • • • •

1 x 400g tin of cannellini beans or butter beans

2 free-range pork chops, on the bone if possible

Salt and freshly ground black pepper

Extra virgin olive oil

100ml white wine

2 sprigs of fresh rosemary

A bunch of fresh sage, roughly torn

1 lemon, halved

1–2 cloves of garlic, peeled but left whole

Preheat the oven to 180°C/fan 160°C/gas mark 4.

Rinse the beans in a sieve or colander.

Season the meat on both sides and brush with some oil.

Heat a heavy-bottomed, ovenproof frying pan until very hot. Brown the meat on all sides, then remove from the pan to a warmed plate.

Add the wine to the frying pan and allow it to bubble up while stirring, thereby deglazing the pan. Add the beans to the pan and return the pork with any juices from the plate.

Add the rosemary and sage, squeeze the lemon juice over the meat and add the lemon halves to the pan.

Place the pan into the oven and cook for 3 minutes, then remove and turn the meat. Spoon the juices in the pan over the meat and return to the oven for a further 2 minutes.

Remove from the oven and let the meat rest for at least 5 minutes before serving. Mash the garlic with a fork in the pan to help it mix through the remaining juices, then spoon these over the meat when serving.

Serve with some steamed greens or tossed leaves.

FLASH MATCHA + MA-YO CRUSTED SALMON

SERVES 4

This dish is from Laura Santtini's book *Flash Cooking*, on which I worked a number of years ago. This is one of my favourite meals from it.

● ● ● ● ● ● ● ● ● ● ● ● ● ● ● ●

Rapeseed oil

4 salmon fillets

Salt and pepper

½ tablespoon low-fat mayonnaise

1½ tablespoons Greek yoghurt

Juice and zest of 1 lime

½ teaspoon matcha green tea

A handful of black sesame seeds (optional)

FOR THE FLASH AGLIO OLIO PEPERONCINO BROWN RICE:

160g short-grain brown rice

4 tablespoons olive oil

3 cloves of garlic, sliced

½ teaspoon chilli flakes

A pinch of salt

2 large handfuls of flat-leaf parsley, chopped

Zest of ½ lemon

1 teaspoon chilli pepper (or more if you like it spicy)

Tenderstem or purple sprouting broccoli, blanched (optional, about 3 stalks per person)

Parmesan cheese, grated

Preheat the oven to 180°C/fan 160°C/gas mark 4.

Cook the rice according to the instructions on the packet until al dente.

While the rice is cooking, brush an ovenproof dish with a little oil to prevent the fish from sticking and place the fillets in it, skin-side down. Season each with a little salt and pepper.

Mix the mayonnaise, yoghurt, lime zest and juice, and matcha tea together in a bowl. Top the fillets with this mixture to make a crust about 5mm (¼ inch) thick.

Cover the dish with foil and place in the oven for 10 minutes, then remove the foil and leave in the oven for a further 5 minutes or until it is golden and bubbling and the fish is cooked through.

While the fish is cooking, prepare the rice. Gently heat the oil in a large non-stick frying pan, then add the garlic, chilli and salt. Cook over a low heat to allow the garlic to flavour the oil. When the garlic is just beginning to colour and puff slightly, remove the pan from the heat – take care not to burn the garlic or it will taste bitter.

Add the well-drained rice, the parsley, lemon zest and chilli pepper to the pan and toss in the garlic-infused oil. If a little dry, add a drizzle more oil. If using the broccoli, mix through the rice.

Serve immediately, sprinkled with the grated Parmesan cheese and accompanied by the salmon, garnished with some black sesame seeds.

75

SALMON TERIYAKI WITH JAPANESE PICKLED CUCUMBER + TOASTED SESAME SEEDS

SERVES 2

You can use shop-bought teriyaki sauce when making this recipe (use 3–4 tablespoons), but I prefer to make my own and that is what I have done in this recipe. It's tastier than the shop-bought equivalent and healthier too, as there are no preservatives or unnatural additives.

• • • • • • • • • • • •

2 salmon fillets

3 tablespoons sesame seeds

FOR THE TERIYAKI SAUCE:

4 tablespoons soy sauce

2 tablespoons rice wine vinegar or mirin (Japanese sweet rice wine)

1 tablespoon honey

1 teaspoon sesame oil

2 tablespoons water mixed with 1½ teaspoons cornflour

2 tablespoons brown sugar

A thumb-sized piece of ginger, finely grated

1 clove of garlic, minced

FOR THE JAPANESE PICKLED CUCUMBER:

½ cucumber

3 tablespoons mirin
(Japanese sweet rice wine)

Start by making the pickled cucumber. Cut the cucumber in half lengthways and scoop out the seeds with a teaspoon. Cut into quarters lengthways. Using a vegetable peeler, slice the cucumber into ribbons. Place in a bowl and douse in the mirin. Leave for at least 1 hour, stirring regularly to ensure the cucumber is fully coated in the mirin.

Mix together all the ingredients for the teriyaki sauce in a pot and bring to the boil. Reduce the heat and simmer until the sauce has thickened (about 3–4 minutes). Ensure the sugar has dissolved.

Heat a frying pan until very hot and fry the salmon on one side for about 2 minutes, turn and cook for the same length of time on the other side. The salmon should be slightly charred and crispy on the outside.

Add the teriyaki sauce to the frying pan with the salmon and reduce the heat. Simmer for about 3–4 minutes until the liquid has thickened and reduced by half.

While the salmon is cooking gently toast the sesame seeds in a dry frying pan.

Serve the salmon with a little of the reduced teriyaki sauce poured over it, accompanied by the oriental rice salad (see p. 79) and Japanese pickled cucumber and with the toasted sesame seeds tossed over it.

SIDES

ORIENTAL RICE SALAD

SERVES 2

100g cooked and cooled rice

2 spring onions, finely sliced

¼ red pepper, finely diced

A small bunch of coriander, roughly torn

FOR THE DRESSING:

1 teaspoon nam pla
(Thai fish sauce)

1 teaspoon soy sauce

Juice of ½ lime

1 teaspoon mirin
(Japanese sweet rice wine)

1 tablespoon brown sugar

This is a great way of using up leftover rice and it gives it a fresh flavour. Use brown rice for a low GI option.

● ● ● ● ● ● ● ● ● ● ●

In a large bowl, mix all the dressing ingredients. Taste and adjust the flavourings to your liking, if necessary.

Add the rice, spring onions, red pepper and coriander and mix thoroughly.

GOAT'S CHEESE, ROAST BEETROOT + WALNUT SALAD WITH ORANGE VANILLA DRESSING

SERVES 2

I love making this salad. The blackberries make this a seasonal dish: buy or pick when they are available. If you can get fresh walnuts (a big ask, I know), it makes this all the better.

• • • • • • • • • • • • • •

1 beetroot

Extra virgin olive oil

120g soft, fresh goat's cheese

½ orange, juiced

1 vanilla pod, seeds removed (or ½ teaspoon vanilla paste if you have it in your store cupboard)

12 blackberries

A handful of whole walnuts

2 large handfuls of baby salad leaves of your choice

Preheat the oven to 180˚C/fan 160˚C/gas mark 4.

To roast the beetroot, gently wash it and trim the tops, leaving a little root. Drizzle a little oil all over it, wrap it up in tinfoil, and place in the oven for about 45 minutes.

When it is just cool enough to handle, peel the skin off using a knife. You may wish to wear rubber gloves to stop your hands staining the colour of the beetroot. Chop the beetroot into bite-sized pieces.

Tear the goat's cheese into smallish chunks.

Make the dressing by mixing together 2 tablespoons of oil, the orange juice and the vanilla seeds. Taste and season.

Place the beetroot, cheese, blackberries, walnuts and baby leaves in a largish bowl. Add the dressing and toss. This is lovely served with edible flowers, such as borage, violas or nasturtiums, on top.

10-MINUTE MEALS

FOR THOSE DAYS WHEN YOU HAVE NO TIME. THE 10 MINUTES IN THIS CHAPTER REFER TO THE LENGTH OF TIME YOU NEED TO PREPARE THESE DISHES, NOT NECESSARILY THE TIME IT TAKES THEM TO COOK.

SPICY CHICKEN BITES WITH COUSCOUS + STEAMED VEG

SERVES 2

½ teaspoon cayenne pepper

½ teaspoon smoked paprika

½ teaspoon allspice

Rapeseed oil

6 mini chicken fillets or 1 large breast of chicken sliced into 6 pieces lengthways

100g barley couscous (or any kind you have)

100ml vegetable or chicken stock

½ red pepper, sliced

A couple of large handfuls of fresh, washed spinach

2–3 sun-dried tomatoes, chopped

½ lemon

A handful of fresh herbs, such as parsley, mint and coriander, roughly chopped

A handful of flaked almonds, toasted

TARA'S TIP:
FOR THE BEST RESULTS WHEN MAKING COUSCOUS I IGNORE PACK INSTRUCTIONS AS I FIND THESE USUALLY LEAVE THE COUSCOUS SOGGY. USE EQUAL QUANTITIES OF LIQUID TO COUSCOUS AND THIS SHOULD BE PERFECT.

I came up with this recipe when I was on a health kick but very short on time. I love using barley couscous for its nutty texture and the fact that it's low GI. Patricia, who works at the cookery school, tested this recipe and got the thumbs up from her husband who's a self-professed plain eater. She also enjoyed it the next day as a salad with some soft goat's cheese and rocket leaves.

• • • • • • • • • • • • •

Mix the spices together in a small bowl, then add a tablespoon of oil. Use a brush to mix this all together, then brush onto the chicken pieces.

Heat a frying pan until very hot and add the chicken, making sure it is all in contact with the pan. You should hear a sizzle as you place the chicken on the pan – if not hold back on placing the rest of the pieces until the first piece starts to sizzle.

In the meantime, prepare the couscous. Place it in the shallowest, widest bowl you have and pour the hot stock over. Cover with cling film or a tea towel and leave for 5 minutes, then fluff up with a fork.

When the chicken is well caramelised and cooked through (this should only take 3–4 minutes), switch the heat off and allow it to rest for a couple of minutes.

When the couscous is ready, toss the pepper, spinach and sun-dried tomatoes through it.

Serve the chicken pieces on top of the couscous with a squeeze of lemon juice and a sprinkling of herbs and almonds.

QUESADILLAS

I suppose this is really just a fancy cheese sandwich, but not so bulky with the tortilla wraps. It is more interesting when jazzed up with some chorizo, spring onion, coriander or any of the other fillings that I have suggested below. My husband often throws this together if I have been on the road late at night, but still fancy a tasty supper. At a minimum, try to serve with sour cream, but a quick salsa, such as the sweetcorn salsa included here, really finishes it beautifully.

SERVES 2

2 tortillas

50g grated cheese

Your choice of fillings (e.g. ham, spring onion, peppers, chilli, leftover chicken, coriander)

1 tablespoon sour cream

FOR THE SWEETCORN SALSA:

100g sweetcorn

1 small red onion, very finely chopped

2 teaspoons white wine vinegar

A glug of olive oil

½ teaspoon sugar

Green chilli or jalapeño pepper, chopped (optional)

Combine all the ingredients for the salsa in a bowl at least 10 minutes before serving to allow the sugar to dissolve and for the flavours to develop a little. Stir well.

Heat a non-stick frying pan over a medium heat and add a tortilla. Sprinkle your filling over it evenly and top with the second tortilla.

Toast gently for a couple of minutes, using a spatula to check the underneath is not burning.

When the cheese has melted, flip the quesadilla over in the pan to toast the other side. Once it is golden brown all over, remove to a chopping board and cut into wedges.

Serve with the salsa and with a dollop of sour cream on top. The tomato salsa on page 95 is also great with these.

LAMB CUTLETS WITH GREEN BEANS, GRIDDLED PEPPERS + BASIL DRESSING

SERVES 4

This is a quick supper that is lovely with a baked potato. The best way to bake a potato is to rub some olive oil onto it, top it with sea salt flakes, then bake it on the shelf in a preheated oven (200°C/180°C fan/gas mark 6) for 45 minutes to 1 hour. I always put my potatoes on a metal skewer, as the metal heats them from the inside out and ensures even cooking.

• • • • • • • • • • • • • •

8 lamb cutlets, with the heavy fat removed

Olive oil

Salt and pepper

250g green beans

1 red pepper, sliced into thick (2 cm) pieces

Juice of ½ lemon

6 fresh basil leaves, roughly torn

1 clove of garlic, minced

Brush the lamb cutlets with some oil and season with salt and pepper.

Heat a griddle pan until smoking and place the cutlets on it. Cook each side for about 2 minutes. Rest on a warm plate.

Add the green beans and pepper to the griddle and reduce the heat. Add a squeeze of lemon juice and a little extra oil if the pan is drying out. Cook for 3–4 minutes, to your liking.

In the meantime, put the basil leaves and garlic in a small bowl, and drizzle with a little olive oil. Add a little lemon juice and salt and pepper to taste and mix together.

Serve the lamb cutlets on top of the vegetables and drizzle with the basil dressing. This is great with a baked potato.

CHICKEN + ORANGE TRAY BAKE WITH GREEN SALAD

This takes 10 minutes to prep, but 30–35 minutes to cook. It is one of those dishes that you can throw in the oven the minute you get in the door. By the time you have changed into something more comfortable and set the table, it will be ready. You could also get it ready the day before and leave it in the fridge, covered, until you are ready to cook it. It is best to use fresh herbs in this recipe, but you can use dried herbs if fresh aren't to hand. I like to use rooster potatoes for this recipe, but other varieties can be used too.

SERVES 4

• • • • • • • • • • • •

8 chicken pieces, a mixture of thighs, drumsticks and skin-on breast on the bone

8 cloves of garlic, peeled but left whole

4 medium-sized potatoes, washed and cut into 1-inch chunks

2 red onions, peeled and cut into wedges

1 courgette, sliced into 2-inch chunks

1 red or yellow pepper, sliced into 2-inch chunks

A few cherry tomatoes

2 sprigs of rosemary, thyme, and oregano

Salt and pepper

2 tablespoons olive oil

1 orange, cut into wedges

1 bag of green salad leaves of your choice

French dressing (see p. 56, make double the amount)

Preheat the oven to 200°C/180°C fan/gas mark 6.

Place the chicken pieces on a large roasting dish and add the garlic, potatoes, vegetables and herbs to the dish. Season with salt and pepper and drizzle with the olive oil, making sure everything is coated. Squeeze a few of the orange wedges over the chicken, then throw all of the wedges in. Make sure the chicken pieces are on top, so that the skin is crispy when cooked.

Roast for 30–35 minutes, checking and stirring every 10 minutes or so to ensure even cooking.

Make the salad dressing.

To serve, divide the chicken, vegetables and potatoes between four plates and drizzle with some of the pan juices. Accompany with the green salad on the side drizzled with the dressing.

GOAT'S CHEESE-STUFFED MUSHROOMS

SERVES 2

75g fresh goat's cheese

2 handfuls of breadcrumbs

Zest of ½ lemon

3 sprigs of flat-leaf parsley, chopped

Black pepper

4 flat-cap or portobello mushrooms

A handy, quick supper for those evenings when you get home late but need a tasty meal!

• • • • • • • • • • •

Preheat the oven to 200°C/fan 180°C/gas mark 6.

In a bowl, mix the goat's cheese with most of the breadcrumbs, lemon zest and parsley with a generous twist of black pepper.

Lay the mushrooms on an ovenproof dish with the stalk removed. Place a quarter of the goat's-cheese mixture on top of each mushroom, in the hole left behind by the stalk. Sprinkle with the remaining breadcrumbs and bake for 5–10 minutes or until the breadcrumbs and goat's cheese are golden.

Serve with a green salad.

COURGETTE + FETA FRITTATA

SERVES 4

I think a frittata is always a great quick supper to throw together, as it is filling and satisfying. This also makes a lovely brunch.

● ● ● ● ● ● ● ● ● ● ● ● ● ●

6 eggs, beaten

100ml cream

Salt and freshly ground black pepper

1 tablespoon rapeseed oil

1 small onion, finely diced

1 medium courgette, thinly sliced

A small handful of mint leaves, chopped

100g feta cheese or soft goat's cheese, chopped roughly

Mix together the eggs and cream with salt and pepper to taste.

Heat the oil in a non-stick frying pan on a medium heat. Add the onion and then the courgette slices with a pinch of salt and fry for 2 minutes.

Pour in the egg mixture, add the mint and stir gently to make sure the courgette slices are spread around evenly.

Sprinkle the cheese on top and cook for 4–5 minutes until the egg mixture is set and brown on the bottom.

Place the pan under the grill for 3–4 minutes, until the frittata is lightly browned and fluffy. Serve immediately with some salad of your choice.

TARA'S TIP:

YOU CAN USE ANY KIND OF LEFTOVER MEAT OR COOKED SALMON IN THE RECIPE, OR LEFTOVER ROAST VEGETABLES. YOU CAN ALSO VARY THE CHEESE, USING WHATEVER YOU HAVE IN THE FRIDGE, SOFT OR HARD.

SPICY TOMATO, OLIVE + BUFFALO MOZZARELLA SPAGHETTI

SERVES 2

I suppose this is a cross between a pasta puttanesca ('lady of the night') and a pasta aglio, olio e peperoncino (garlic, oil and chilli pepper). Mini mozzarella balls (use about 10) are very useful for this recipe as well. I've only added a handful of olives here, but if you love olives feel free to go mad! I love spelt spaghetti in this dish.

• • • • • • • • • • • • • • • •

100g spaghetti

Olive oil

1 clove of garlic (thinly sliced)

2 anchovies (optional)

A large handful of Kalamata olives, stoned

1 teaspoon dried chilli flakes

A few cherry tomatoes, halved

1 buffalo mozzarella, sliced in ½cm discs

2 sprigs of flat-leaf parsley or basil

Cook the spaghetti according to the pack instructions until al dente.

Gently heat a good glug of oil in a large frying pan and add the garlic, anchovies (if using), olives, chilli flakes and cherry tomatoes. Cook until the garlic has softened a little and the anchovy has started to dissolve (2–3 minutes). Toss the spaghetti through the sauce until it is well coated.

Toss the slices of mozzarella through the spaghetti and serve with the fresh herbs sprinkled over the top.

TUNA STEAKS WITH TOMATO SALSA

SERVES 4

This is very popular at my cooking classes as it is so simple but so tasty and refreshing. Make sure not to overcook the tuna! If you can't get fresh tuna steaks, this is also lovely with pork steaks. Simply cut them into ½-inch slices and proceed as per the recipe.

● ● ● ● ● ● ● ● ● ● ● ●

4 tuna steaks

Groundnut or rapeseed oil

1 bag of rocket or mixed leaves

FOR THE TOMATO SALSA:

2 large tomatoes, chopped, or 10 cherry tomatoes, cut in half

1 clove of garlic, minced

½ red onion, finely chopped

1 teaspoon sugar

2 tablespoons red wine vinegar

A handful of fresh coriander, chopped

A pinch of sea salt

Make the salsa by combining all the ingredients in a bowl, then set aside.

Heat a griddle pan until it is good and hot, almost smoking.

Brush the tuna steaks with a good glug of oil and place in the griddle pan. Cook on each side for 1–2 minutes depending on how thick they are. They should be served rare or medium rare.

Remove the tuna to warmed plates and serve with the tomato salsa, some rocket or mixed leaves and potato wedges (see p. 72).

DITCH THE TAKE-AWAY

THIS CHAPTER IS FOR A TYPICAL FRIDAY NIGHT WHEN YOU WANT TO LAZE ON THE COUCH, MAYBE WITH A COLD BEER. ALL OF THESE RECIPES HAVE A LITTLE SPICE AND PLENTY OF FLAVOUR TO SATISFY THAT FRIDAY NIGHT FEELING. NOW I KNOW THESE TAKE MORE EFFORT THAN SIMPLY DIALLING THE TAKE-AWAY, BUT THE RECIPES ARE ALL QUITE HEALTHY, NOURISHING AND PROBABLY CHEAPER. FOR ME, GETTING A TAKE-AWAY ISN'T REALLY AN OPTION, BECAUSE WE LIVE IN THE COUNTRYSIDE, SO THESE RECIPES TICK THAT BOX.

ONION BHAJIS WITH INDIAN-STYLE DIPPING YOGHURT

SERVES 4

If you're having a take-away night and fancy pushing out the boat and having a starter, there is nothing like a homemade bhaji. They are fantastic and fabulous and only take 10 minutes to make. Everyone who tastes these at my classes finds it hard to believe the difference between them and the mass-produced versions.

• • • • • • • • • • • • • • • •

150g gram flour

1 teaspoon salt

1 teaspoon bicarbonate of soda

1 teaspoon cumin seeds

1 teaspoon fennel seeds

200ml water

2 large onions, sliced thinly in semi-circles

2 sprigs of coriander, leaves removed

Sunflower oil for frying

FOR THE INDIAN-STYLE DIPPING YOGHURT:

3 tablespoons Greek yoghurt

1 teaspoon turmeric

A squeeze of lime juice

Sieve the flour into a large bowl and add the salt, bicarbonate of soda, cumin and fennel seeds. Mix together.

Gradually add the water and whisk until you have a thick batter.

Add the onions and coriander and combine.

Heat a generous amount of oil in a frying pan. Using 2 teaspoons (so the mixture doesn't fall all over the place) place small heaps of the mixture into the oil. When golden brown on the underside turn over and cook for another 2–3 minutes until golden brown. Remove and drain on kitchen paper.

To make the dipping yoghurt, combine all the ingredients. If you feel this needs seasoning then you can add a pinch of sea salt.

Serve the bhajis with the yoghurt dip and a little mango chutney, if you have it.

CHICKEN TANDOORI POCKETS

SERVES 4

This is a perfect tea-time meal. It is quick and tasty but also very satisfying. You don't have to make the tandoori paste from scratch, but most of the ingredients are store cupboard stand-bys and if you make your own, then you know there are no nasty hidden ingredients in it.

• • • • • • • • • • • • •

100g natural yoghurt

1 teaspoon lime juice, plus extra for squeezing

2 large chicken fillets, sliced into strips (about 6 per fillet)

Rapeseed oil

1 portion of raita (see p. 58)

4 pitta pockets or tortilla wraps

2 handfuls of young lettuce leaves

1 fresh red chilli, sliced thinly

A handful of freshly chopped coriander

FOR THE TANDOORI PASTE:

1 tablespoon ground cumin

1 teaspoon ground coriander

2 cloves of garlic, grated

1 teaspoon chilli flakes

1 teaspoon turmeric

1 teaspoon tomato purée

A thumb-sized piece of ginger, grated

To make the tandoori paste, simply combine all the ingredients in a small bowl.

Place the natural yoghurt into a bowl, then add the tandoori paste and 1 teaspoon of lime juice. Combine well.

Place the chicken in a bowl and pour the tandoori marinade over it, making sure the sauce completely covers the chicken.

Heat a large frying pan or griddle, add a little oil and cook the chicken in batches, turning once. Check the chicken is cooked after about 5 minutes by slicing the thickest piece in the middle.

Allow the meat to rest while you make the raita and toast the pitta pockets or warm the tortillas on a dry frying pan.

To serve, place some of the lettuce leaves into your chosen wrapping, followed by some of the chicken and the chilli. Top with some raita and coriander and squeeze over a little lime juice. Roll up the wrap (if using) and enjoy.

LAMB + FETA BURGERS

These are my take on lamb koftas. If you can't be bothered making the raita, just pop a couple of dollops of natural or Greek yoghurt on when you are serving. These burgers can also be cooked on the barbecue. I like to serve the burgers in lightly toasted pitta breads as they are lighter than burger buns, but if you prefer the traditional bun, go for it.

SERVES 4

450g lamb mince

1 red onion, chopped

1 clove of garlic, finely chopped

2 tablespoons fresh oregano (use 1 teaspoon of dried if you don't have fresh)

1 tablespoon finely chopped fresh parsley

1 preserved lemon, finely chopped

1 teaspoon ground cumin

100g feta cheese, crumbled

1 egg, whisked lightly

Salt and pepper

1 portion of raita (see p. 58)

Pitta bread

Rocket leaves

Combine the lamb mince, red onion, garlic, oregano, parsley, lemon, cumin and feta in a bowl with half of the egg, keeping the other half back. Mix thoroughly and check that the mix is wet enough to hold together – add more egg if necessary. Season the mixture and cook a teaspoonful of it to check that it is seasoned the way you like it.

Once you are happy with the flavour, shape into patties and refrigerate if time allows, as this helps the burgers to keep their shape.

Cook on a griddle or pan for 5–8 minutes on each side, checking the middle of one to ensure it is cooked through.

Leave to rest for 5 minutes and make the raita.

Place each burger in a pitta with some raita and rocket leaves.

TARA'S TIP:

THIS BURGER RECIPE CAN ALSO BE USED FOR MEATBALLS, WHICH ARE GREAT BAKED IN THE TOMATO SAUCE ON PAGE 222.

GOAN FISH MASALA

Making your own curry paste for the first time is a real revelation. I often include a curry paste as a recipe during my cookery lessons. People who have always used shop-bought curry pastes are usually amazed at the fragrance achieved with a freshly made curry paste. There are many different types of curry pastes from all over the East and Far East and I love playing around with different ingredients. Curry paste keeps well in the fridge for up to four weeks, as long as the surface is covered with oil. It is a great standby as it can be used in a stir-fry for a quick meal that is full of flavour.

SERVES 4

• • • • • • • • • • • • • •

1 tablespoon Goan curry paste (see p. 58)

Groundnut oil

1 large onion, sliced thinly in semi-circles

Salt

500ml fish stock

500g mixed fish, e.g. haddock, trout, salmon, cod

150g baby sweetcorn, whole

A handful of spinach leaves, washed

2 tablespoons coconut cream

A handful of fresh coriander, roughly chopped

A handful of flaked almonds, toasted gently on a dry pan

Make the curry paste and set aside.

Heat a heavy-based saucepan and add a glug of the groundnut oil. Add the onion with a pinch of salt and sweat with a lid on for a few minutes until softened.

Add 1 tablespoon of the curry paste (use more or less if you like it more or less spicy) and cook for a couple of minutes. Then add the fish stock and simmer for 15–20 minutes.

Add the fish pieces and baby sweetcorn and cook for about 5 minutes, then add the spinach and the coconut cream to thicken the sauce, cooking for a further minute or so. Be careful not to overcook the fish or it will become dry.

Garnish with the coriander and some toasted flaked almonds and serve with the spiced pilau rice on page 116.

VIETNAMESE SPRING ROLLS

20 prawns (I recommend buying Dublin Bay prawn tails),
or 2 chicken fillets, sliced into bite-sized pieces

1 large piece of ginger, peeled and sliced

1 tablespoon nam pla
(Thai fish sauce)

1 fresh red chilli, sliced

6 spring onions

500ml chicken or vegetable stock

1 portion rice noodles

½ cucumber

1 large carrot

A few sprigs of fresh coriander and mint

A few handfuls of beansprouts

1 packet of Vietnamese rice-paper wrappers

FOR THE ASIAN DRESSING:

1–2 limes, juiced

2 tablespoons nam pla

2 tablespoons brown sugar

1 fresh red chilli, deseeded and finely chopped

1 clove of garlic, minced

A thumb-sized piece of ginger, peeled and grated

These are fantastic, healthy and tasty little rolls. They are quick to prepare and are perfect for a midweek meal as well as if you have a craving for a Chinese on a Friday evening. If you don't want to bother putting these into rice paper, which can be a little fiddly, you can just eat the filling as a nutritious salad instead. It can also be a bit of fun if you serve all the ingredients on a platter or lazy Susan and allow diners to make up their own rolls. If doing so, serve a dipping sauce in small bowls. You can make these a little ahead of time and keep them in the fridge covered with a piece of damp kitchen roll or tea towel.

• • • • • • • • • • • • •

Combine all the ingredients for the dressing in a bowl and set aside. The sugar has to be completely dissolved before this is ready to use.

If using the prawns, squeeze them to break the shell and pull the shell off at the tail end, taking the entrails with it.

Place the shelled prawns or chicken pieces, slices of ginger, nam pla, chilli and two of the spring onions, roughly sliced, in a pot and cover with the stock. Bring to the boil.

Remove the meat from the pot as soon as it is cooked: if cooking prawns, this should take about 1 minute; the chicken pieces will take 3–4 minutes longer. Put in a colander to cool. If using prawns, chop each in half. Discard the stock and the flavourings.

Cook the noodles as per the instructions on the pack, then rinse with cold water and drain well.

Finely slice the cucumber, the remaining spring onions and the carrot (use a mandolin if possible) into matchstick-sized pieces and roughly chop the herbs. Wash the beansprouts and trim if desired.

Fill a large bowl with lukewarm water and place the discs of rice paper into the bowl two at a time. Submerge for about 2 minutes or until softened, then remove. I recommend keeping the rice papers in a clean, damp tea towel whilst you are waiting to fill them as they dry out very quickly.

Put the chicken or prawns, noodles, vegetables and herbs into a large bowl, add the dressing and toss.

Place a spoonful of the filling along the middle of each rice-paper roll. Tuck in the ends of the ricepaper, roll up and enjoy.

HOMEMADE FISH + CHIPS

SERVES 4

My husband (a Yorkshire man) says that no chapter on ditching the take-away could be complete without including fish and chips. So here's a slightly healthier version with homemade ketchup! For me, rooster potatoes make the best chips, but if they're not available other varieties can be used.

• • • • • • • • • • • • •

Olive oil

4 large rooster potatoes

Salt and pepper

100g breadcrumbs

75ml milk

1 egg

3 tablespoons plain flour

300g fresh fish fillet, skinned (haddock, hake, cod, etc.)

FOR THE HOMEMADE KETCHUP:

75ml red wine vinegar

½ teaspoon ground coriander

½ teaspoon ground cinnamon

25g brown sugar

1 fresh bay leaf

1 x 400g can tinned tomatoes

1 teaspoon salt

1 teaspoon English mustard powder

1 clove of garlic, crushed

Tabasco sauce, to taste

2 teaspoons tomato purée

1 tablespoon cornflour mixed to a paste with 1 tablespoon water (optional)

Preheat the oven to 180°C/fan 160°C/gas mark 4.

Pour some olive oil into a roasting dish and place in the oven. Peel the potatoes and cut into chip-sized pieces.

Put the potatoes into the well-heated roasting dish (you should hear a sizzle!), sprinkle with salt and pepper and coat with the heated oil. Be careful not to burn your hands!

Cook for 20–30 minutes or until soft on the inside and crisp on the outside.

When the potatoes are in the oven, set up three bowls or plates. Place the breadcrumbs in one, the milk mixed with the egg in another, and in the last put the flour seasoned with salt and pepper.

Make sure your fish is nice and dry, using kitchen roll to dry it if necessary. Slice into goujons.

Dip the fish into the flour, followed by the egg and milk, and then the breadcrumbs. Place in an ovenproof dish and bake for about 20 minutes, until crispy and cooked through. The time will depend on the thickness of the fillets of fish.

To make the homemade ketchup, heat the vinegar, coriander, cinnamon and sugar in a heavy-based saucepan until simmering.

Add the remaining ingredients, except the cornflour, and bring to the boil, stirring to prevent the mixture from sticking to the side of the pan. Once the mixture has reached boiling point, reduce the temperature to a simmer and cook for a further 6–8 minutes, stirring occasionally.

Remove the bay leaf, then blend the mixture in a blender until smooth. Push the blended mixture through a sieve into a bowl.

If the mixture is a little thin, whisk the cornflour mixture into the ketchup and heat through until the mixture has thickened. Season with salt and freshly ground black pepper.

When everything is ready, serve the fish and chips with the ketchup on the side.

HOMEMADE PIZZA WITH CARAMELISED ONION, POTATO, BELLINGHAM BLUE CHEESE + THYME

**MAKES 1 LARGE OR
4 X 6-INCH PIZZAS**

A cross between a pizza bianca (no tomato sauce) and its French neighbour, pissaladière (a delicious tart similar to a pizza, topped with well-caramelised onions, originating in Nice in the south of France).

• • • • • • • • • • • • •

FOR THE BASE:

325g plain or strong white flour

7g pack fast-acting yeast

1½ tablespoons olive oil

175–200ml lukewarm water

½ tablespoon sugar

½ teaspoon salt

FOR THE TOPPING:

1 potato

1 tablespoon olive oil

1 knob of butter

1 onion, thinly sliced

A pinch of salt

100g Bellingham blue cheese, in chunks

A couple of sprigs of thyme, leaves removed

Put the flour into a large bowl. Make a well in the centre, add the yeast and the oil and about 2 tablespoons of the water. Add the sugar and salt on top of the flour, trying to keep the salt away from the yeast initially, as it can kill the yeast before it has a chance to activate. Gradually work the water and oil into the flour, then add the rest of the water bit by bit, working it in to make a soft dough. Sprinkle in a little extra flour if the mixture feels too sticky, but make sure it is not too dry – the dough should be pliable and smooth.

Transfer the dough to a lightly floured work surface, knead for 10 minutes (sprinkling a little flour on the work surface when needed) until the dough is smooth and stretchy (soft but elastic).

Shape the dough into a ball, stretching the top by gently tucking any rough edges into the centre on the bottom of the ball. Place the rounded dough into a lightly oiled bowl; cover with plastic wrap and let it rise in a warm spot until double in volume – this should take about 1 to 1½ hours. Check it after 1 hour – the dough is ready when it does not spring back when a finger is poked into it.

While the dough is rising, boil the potato for a couple of minutes, then slice thinly. If you use a mandolin for slicing the potato there is no need to boil it.

To make the topping add the oil and butter to a frying pan, then add the onion and salt and caramelise for at least 10 minutes, stirring occasionally. You want the onion to be a deep-brown colour.

Preheat the oven to 220°C/fan 200°C/gas mark 7 and heat a baking sheet in the oven.

Gently remove the dough to a floured surface and dust your hands with flour. For one pizza, use all of the dough, or using a knife, divide it into four pieces, for four individual pizzas. To shape the dough, using your fingertips begin pushing the dough from the centre out towards the edge and then start pulling, stretching and turning the piece of dough in the air to make it thinner and thinner without making a hole. Remember that the more you handle the dough, the tougher it becomes.

Top with the onion followed by the slices of potato, the cheese and the thyme leaves.

Bake in the oven for about 10 minutes or until golden brown on top.

TARA'S TIP:

THE BASIC PIZZA-BASE RECIPE HERE CAN BE TOPPED WITH WHATEVER YOU LIKE. IF YOU PREFER A TOMATO BASE ON YOUR PIZZA, THEN JUST USE THE TOMATO SAUCE RECIPE ON PAGE 222.

CHICKEN KIEV

SERVES 4

One of my childhood favourites and now one of my daughter's too. This is a great alternative to fried chicken take-away.

• ● • ● • ● • ● • ● • ● • ●

2 cloves of garlic, crushed

A small bunch of flat-leaf parsley, chopped

100g butter

A squeeze of lemon juice

Salt and black pepper

4 chicken fillets

1 egg

A drop of milk

100g plain flour

A few large handfuls of breadcrumbs

3 tablespoons rapeseed oil

For the garlic butter, combine the garlic, parsley, butter and lemon juice and season to taste.

Place your chicken breast on a board lengthways. At the fattest part, run your knife along it to open it and butterfly it out. Place a quarter of the garlic butter in the centre of one side of the chicken and then close it back over.

Place the egg and milk in a large shallow bowl and mix. Place the flour in another bowl and the breadcrumbs in another.

Place the chicken in the flour and coat both sides, shaking off the excess. Dip the coated chicken in the egg and then in the breadcrumbs, making sure that it is evenly covered.

Heat the oil until piping hot in a frying pan. To check the oil is hot enough, throw a few breadcrumbs in – if they sizzle straight away, you are good to go.

Using a large slotted spoon or tongs, place the chicken into the oil carefully. Turn the chicken round in the oil every couple of minutes or so until it is evenly cooked on the outside and golden crisp. It will take about ten minutes in total. Ensure the chicken is fully cooked in the centre by cutting it in half before serving.

Serve with homemade chips (see p. 108) or if you prefer something spicier, spiced cauliflower and potatoes (see p. 117).

SIDES

SPICED PILAU RICE

The job of the cardamom, cloves and cinnamon here is to make the rice gorgeous and fragrant. I always leave them in to serve because I think they look pretty. But tell your guests not to eat them!

• • • • • • • • • • • • •

225g basmati rice

5 green cardamom pods

30g ghee or 2 tablespoons groundnut oil

5 cloves

½ cinnamon stick

1 teaspoon fennel seeds

½ teaspoon black mustard seeds

2 bay leaves

450ml water

1½ teaspoon salt, and extra to season

Pepper

Rinse the basmati rice in several changes of water until the water runs clear, then drain and set aside until ready to cook.

Bash the cardamon pods a couple of times in a pestle and mortar to release the seeds.

Melt the ghee in or add the oil to a flameproof casserole dish or large saucepan with a tight-fitting lid over a medium to high heat. Add the spices and bay leaves and stir for 30 seconds. Stir the rice into the casserole so the grains are coated with the ghee/oil. Stir in the water and salt and bring to the boil.

Reduce the heat to as low as possible and cover the dish/saucepan tightly. Simmer without lifting the lid for 8–10 minutes, until the rice is tender and all the liquid is absorbed.

Turn off the heat and use two forks to fluff up the rice. Adjust the seasoning, adding salt and pepper if necessary. Cover the pan again and leave to stand for 5 minutes.

SPICED CAULIFLOWER + POTATOES

SERVES 4

A delicious side dish well worth making.

• • • • • • • • • • • •

3 large potatoes, peeled and diced

1 head of cauliflower, chopped into small florets

Sunflower oil

1 clove of garlic, finely chopped

1 teaspoon turmeric

Salt to taste

FOR THE PANCH PHORON:

½ teaspoon nigella seeds

½ teaspoon fenugreek

½ teaspoon fennel seeds

½ teaspoon black mustard seeds

½ teaspoon cumin seeds

Mix all the ingredients of the panch phoron together and set aside.

Boil the potatoes until al dente and drain, then do the same with the cauliflower.

Add a little sunflower oil to a frying pan over a medium heat. Add the potatoes and cauliflower and sauté for a few minutes until they start to turn golden.

Push the potatoes and cauliflower to the sides of the pan and add 1 tablespoon of the panch phoron to the centre. Allow the seeds to start popping. Once they do, add the garlic, turmeric and salt to taste, and stir all the ingredients together. Cook until the garlic is golden. Taste and if necessary add more seasoning.

FAST
FRESH FISH

· · · · · · · · · · · · · · · · · ·

LIVING ON THE EAST COAST, CLOSE TO THE FISHING VILLAGE
OF CLOGHERHEAD, WE ARE VERY LUCKY TO HAVE ACCESS
TO GREAT FRESH FISH. I THINK FISH IS THE ULTIMATE
HEALTHY FAST FOOD. I EAT IT TWO TO THREE EVENINGS A
WEEK AND I NEVER TIRE OF TRYING NEW WAYS TO BOTH
COOK AND FLAVOUR IT. WHAT FOLLOWS IS A SELECTION
OF MY FAVOURITE AND EASIEST FISH DISHES.

CRAB CLAWS IN A GARLIC CREAM SAUCE

SERVES 2

Olive oil

1 clove of garlic, finely chopped

Salt

12 crab claws, cooked

100ml whipping cream

Juice of ½ lemon

Some parsley, finely chopped

My dad made this starter in his restaurant for years, so I couldn't bear not to put it in here. This is pretty much the exact recipe from the late 1980s – why mess with a classic?

• • • • • • • • • • • • •

Place a little oil into a frying pan and heat to medium. Place the chopped garlic in the pan with a little salt. Cook for a moment and then add the crab claws. Toss the claws in the garlic.

Add the cream and allow to bubble up for a few minutes until it is thickened. Avoid stirring. Add a squeeze of lemon juice and the parsley. Serve immediately in small bowls or ramekins, or on a platter and let everyone dive in. This is lovely served with the Guinness Brown Bread on page 149.

SCALLOP CEVICHE

This recipe uses the ultimate summer flavours! It works well either as a starter or as a light supper with some crusty bread. I beg you not to be nervous about eating what may seem like raw fish – the acid in the citrus juices 'cooks' the scallops. It is vital to get fresh scallops for this.

• • • • • • • • • • • •

SERVES 2

6 fresh scallops, sliced very thinly

Juice of 1 lime

Juice of ½ lemon

A pinch of sea salt

1 ripe tomato, skinned and chopped

1 red chilli, chopped

½ red onion, chopped

1 avocado, cubed

A handful of fresh coriander, chopped

Lay the scallop slices out on a platter and pour lime and lemon juice over them. Sprinkle with a pinch of salt and leave in the fridge to marinade for at least 2 hours.

When they are ready to serve, remove them from the fridge and scatter the tomato, chilli, red onion and avocado over the top. Then sprinkle with the coriander and serve.

INDIAN–STYLE MACKEREL WITH GOOSEBERRY CHUTNEY + GRAPE SALAD

SERVES 2

This dish was inspired by a stunning Atul Kochhar 'Mackerel Rechado' recipe I once assisted him with at Taste of Dublin, if a lot simpler!

• • • • • • • • • • • • •

4 mackerel, filleted, pin bones removed

10 green grapes

1 teaspoon lime juice

A handful of fresh coriander, chopped

½ teaspoon toasted cumin seeds, lightly toasted in a dry frying pan, then crushed

1 teaspoon olive oil

FOR THE SPICE PASTE:

½ teaspoon ground cumin

¼ teaspoon cardamom powder

½ teaspoon cinnamon

½ teaspoon turmeric

¼ teaspoon allspice

½ teaspoon chilli flakes

FOR THE GOOSEBERRY CHUTNEY:

2 tablespoons rapeseed oil

1 teaspoon panch phoron (see p. 117)

75g gooseberries

20ml red wine vinegar

1 tablespoon brown sugar

Salt to taste

First make the chutney. Heat the oil in a frying pan over a high heat. Add the panch phoron and sauté until it crackles.

Add the gooseberries, vinegar, sugar and salt. Reduce the heat and simmer for 10–15 minutes until the fruit is cooked. The gooseberries should be completely soft and sticky. Set aside to cool.

Mix all the ingredients for the spice paste together in a bowl. Smear the paste well over the fish fillets. Place the fish into a lightly oiled, ovenproof dish and cook it in a hot oven for 7–10 minutes, or alternatively heat a thin layer of oil in a large frying pan, add the mackerel and fry for about 2–3 minutes on each side, until just cooked through.

Mix the grapes, lime juice, coriander, cumin seeds and olive oil together and toss well.

Serve the fish with the salad and chutney on the side.

CHERMOULA BAKED HAKE WITH LIME YOGHURT DRESSING

SERVES 4

This recipe is what I would like to call a great return on your investment, i.e. you get a great dish for very little effort. This is a favourite from my 'Foods of North Africa and Middle East' class.

• • • • • • • • • • • •

2 cloves of garlic, minced

2 teaspoons ground cumin

2 teaspoons ground coriander

1 teaspoon chilli flakes

1 teaspoon paprika

1 tablespoon preserved lemon skin, finely chopped

½ teaspoon sea salt

Olive oil

4 fillets of hake (or any other white fish)

A handful of flat-leaf parsley, roughly chopped

FOR THE YOGHURT DRESSING:

2 tablespoons Greek yoghurt

1 clove of garlic, minced

Juice of ½ lime

Salt and pepper

Preheat the oven to 180°C/fan 160°C/gas mark 4.

To make the chermoula marinade, mix together the garlic, cumin, coriander, chilli, paprika, preserved lemon, salt and a good glug of olive oil.

Place the fish into a lightly oiled baking dish and pour over the marinade. Cover the dish with tinfoil and bake for 20–30 minutes, depending on the thickness of your fish.

To make sure it is cooked, gently open a piece of the fish with a knife and check the flesh is opaque.

To make the yoghurt dressing, place the yoghurt in a bowl with the garlic and lime juice, and mix. Season to taste.

Serve the fish in the sauce with the yoghurt dressing drizzled over it and garnished with the parsley. This is great with the tabbouleh on page 184.

CLASSIC PRAWN COCKTAIL

SERVES 2

Another classic starter recipe from my parents' restaurant in the 1980s. For a really retro presentation halve an avocado and place the prawns and Marie Rose sauce in the centre where the stone was.

• • • • • • • • • • • • •

12 Dublin Bay prawns or langoustines

1 tablespoon mayonnaise

¼ teaspoon tomato purée

A few drops of Worcestershire sauce

A few drops of Tabasco

½ teaspoon cayenne pepper

½ lemon

Salt

¼ head of iceberg lettuce, washed and very thinly sliced

1 avocado, peeled and diced

⅓ cucumber cut into four lengthways and thinly sliced

Place the prawns in a pot and cover with cold water. Bring to the boil, then remove to a colander immediately. They should have just turned opaque and be a pinkish colour. Be careful not to overcook them.

Make the Marie Rose sauce by combining the mayonnaise, tomato purée, Worcestershire sauce, Tabasco and cayenne pepper in a bowl with a squeeze of lemon juice and salt to taste. Mix, then taste and add more seasoning if required. Set aside until you are ready to use.

To serve, I usually place equal portions of the shredded iceberg lettuce in the bottom of two tall cocktail glasses, followed by the avocado and cucumber. Top this with the prawns and a generous tablespoon of Marie Rose sauce and sprinkle with a little extra cayenne pepper. Garnish with a slice of lemon.

This is lovely served with the Guinness Brown Bread on page 149.

NO-CARB FISH CAKES

SERVES 4
AS A LIGHT SUPPER

These fish cakes are a great canapé, lunch or light supper. I love the fact that there are no potatoes or breadcrumbs in them and it's just all fish. My daughter loves these inside a toasted wholemeal wrap.

• • • • • • • • • • • • •

200g skinless white fish fillets (such as cod or haddock)

2 teaspoons harissa

1 teaspoon ground cumin

1 tablespoon fresh lime juice

1 preserved lemon, pips removed

1 thumb-sized piece of ginger, grated

1 small egg, beaten

A small bunch of fresh coriander, chopped

2 tablespoons rapeseed oil

FOR THE CHILLI CRÈME FRAÎCHE:

2 tablespoons crème fraîche

4 tablespoons sweet chilli sauce

Slice the fish into chunks and put it into a food processor with the rest of the ingredients, excluding the oil and holding some of the egg back. Blitz for about 10 seconds. Check the mixture has bound together and add more egg if necessary and blitz again.

Divide the mixture into about eight cakes and shape into flattened rounds.

Heat a frying pan and add the oil. Fry the fish cakes over a medium heat in batches for 3–4 minutes on each side. When they are golden brown, drain on kitchen paper.

To make the chilli crème fraîche, combine the ingredients well.

Serve the fish cakes with a few green salad leaves and the chilli crème fraîche on the side.

ZUPPA DI PESCE (FISH SOUP) WITH SAFFRON AIOLI

SERVES 4

2 tablespoons olive oil

2 shallots, finely chopped

A pinch of dried chilli flakes

1 clove of garlic, finely chopped

Salt

1 glass of white wine

1 x 400g tin of chopped tomatoes

200ml water

1 teaspoon sugar

400g mixed fish and shellfish of your choice (I use Clogher Head hake and cod)

FOR THE SAFFRON AIOLI:

A pinch of saffron

2 tablespoons mayonnaise

1 clove of garlic, minced

½ lemon

In my 'Fish landed in Clogherhead' class we do a traditional bouillabaisse-style fish stew, but in the 'Italian Kitchen' class we make this zuppa di pesce with saffron aioli, which is much faster and easier, and I actually prefer it!

• • • • • • • • • • • • •

Heat the oil and gently sauté the shallots, dried chilli flakes and garlic with some salt. Add the white wine and bubble for a few minutes to deglaze the pan.

Add the tomatoes, water and sugar and simmer for at least 5 minutes. Then add the fish to the pan and continue cooking until it is cooked through (about 5 minutes – be careful not to overcook it).

While the fish is cooking, make the aioli. Toast the saffron in a pan for 1–2 minutes over a medium heat until fragrant, then grind down into a powder in a pestle and mortar. Mix with the mayonnaise, garlic and a squeeze of lemon juice.

Ladle the soup into bowls and serve with the aioli spooned on top.

TARA'S TIP:

YOU CAN MAKE A NICE VEGETARIAN SOUP WITH A SIMILAR RECIPE. CUBE AND ROAST SOME BUTTERNUT SQUASH IN SOME OLIVE OIL, SALT AND PEPPER AT 180°C/FAN 160°C/GAS MARK 4 UNTIL SOFT AND GOLDEN (ABOUT 20 MINUTES). ADD THIS TO THE SOUP BASE INSTEAD OF THE FISH, ALONG WITH SOME CANNELLINI OR BUTTER BEANS AND PROCEED AS ABOVE.

CRISPY SZECHUAN SQUID WITH PONZU SAUCE

SERVES 2

One of my all-time favourite fish dishes. Please, please do not let the fact that it is squid turn you off. You can ask your fishmonger to prepare it for you – just ask them to score the body and leave the tentacles whole. The ponzu sauce is a cinch, no cooking involved.

• • • • • • • • • • • • • • • •

1 tablespoon Sichuan peppercorns

A large handful of spinach or chard, washed

3 tablespoons plain flour

Salt

2–3 large squid, cleaned out (your fishmonger should do this for you)

3 tablespoons groundnut oil

FOR THE PONZU SAUCE:

1 clove of garlic, finely chopped or minced

Juice of 1 lime

Juice of ½ lemon

1 tablespoon soy sauce

1 tablespoon mirin

1 tablespoon rice wine vinegar

2 strands of dried seaweed – wakame or dulse works well (optional)

TO GARNISH (OPTIONAL):

1 teaspoon black sesame seeds

1 red chilli, sliced

1 spring onion, finely chopped

A handful of fresh coriander, chopped

To make the ponzu sauce, mix all the ingredients together and leave aside for the flavours to infuse.

Toast the Sichuan peppercorns on a dry frying pan, then grind down in a pestle and mortar, spice grinder or coffee grinder.

Using the same frying pan, place the greens onto the still-hot pan with a small drop of water and allow to wilt down. Remove from the pan and keep warm until ready to serve.

Place the flour on a plate and season with salt and most of the Sichuan pepper, reserving a little for later.

Dry off the squid, and open out the body by cutting along one side. Score a diamond pattern onto the inside part of the body. Dip the body and tentacles into the flour and shake off any excess.

Place the oil in a pan and heat until very hot, then add the squid. Cook on each side until starting to become golden brown. This should take 3–4 minutes in total. Drain on kitchen paper.

Before serving, strain the ponzu sauce to ensure it is nice and smooth. Then pour it around a plate and top with the wilted greens and the squid. Garnish with the black sesame seeds, chilli, spring onion and coriander.

PAN-FRIED JOHN DORY WITH GREEN BEANS, CANNELLINI BEANS + LEMON THYME

Cannellini beans are a handy store cupboard stand-by. They are full of protein and therefore filling. You will thank me when it is time to do the washing up as this is a one-pan dish. For a better flavour buy the Kalamata olives with the stones in and remove them yourself.

SERVES 2

• • • • • • • • • • • • • •

2 fillets of John Dory (or other white fish such as turbot or brill)

1 tablespoon plain flour

Salt and pepper

4 tablespoons olive oil (approx.)

3 cloves of garlic, thinly sliced

A handful of fresh lemon thyme leaves (use ordinary thyme if not available)

Zest and juice of 1 lemon

A pinch of dried chilli flakes

A large handful of green beans (blanched if they are a bit hard)

10 good-quality Kalamata olives

1 x 400g tin of cannellini beans, drained and rinsed

A knob of butter

1–2 tablespoons soy sauce (optional)

A handful of fresh parsley, chopped

Dry the fillets of fish with kitchen paper and sprinkle lightly with the flour and some salt and pepper, shaking gently to remove the excess.

Heat a non-stick frying pan until very hot. Add 1 table-spoon of oil and the butter and, when the butter is foaming, add the fillets of John Dory, flesh-side down. Cook until the flesh has turned a nice golden brown, then turn over. The fish will rise up in the middle when it is ready – this will not take long. It is important not to overcook the fish. Remove to a warm plate to rest.

Wipe the frying pan with a piece of kitchen roll, then heat the rest of the oil in the pan over a very gentle heat. Add the garlic, lemon thyme, lemon zest and chilli. After about 2 minutes and keeping the pan on a very low heat, add the green beans, olives and cannellini beans and cook for 2–3 minutes more, until the beans are warmed through.

Add the soy sauce (if using – this will depend on taste), a squeeze of lemon juice and the chopped parsley to the beans. Taste and adjust the seasoning if needed.

Place equal portions of the beans on two plates with a fillet of fish on top.

TOMATO, PARMESAN + COURGETTE CRUNCHY FISH BAKE

SERVES 4

This recipe could be in the 'Cooking with Kids' chapter, as all the kids who come to our cookery camps love it and it's so easy to make.

• • • • • • • • • • • • • •

2 tablespoons tomato purée

1 x 400g tin of tomatoes

1 teaspoon sugar

1 teaspoon soy sauce

Salt and pepper

100ml water

600g mixed fish

1 courgette, sliced

A handful of flat-leaf parsley, chopped

75g breadcrumbs

50g Parmesan, grated

A good knob of butter

A bag of mixed leaves

Preheat the oven to 160°C/fan 140°C/gas mark 3.

To make the sauce, place the tomato purée in a pan over a medium heat. Cook for a moment, then add the tin of tomatoes, whisking. Add the sugar, soy sauce, a pinch of salt and pepper and water and allow to bubble for a couple of minutes.

Place the fish in an ovenproof dish with the courgette and parsley. Pour the sauce over the fish, scatter the breadcrumbs and Parmesan over the top, and dab the butter on in five or six places.

Bake for 25 minutes or until the fish is cooked through. Serve with dressed mixed leaves.

HAKE TACO CUPS WITH GUACAMOLE + SALSA

SERVES 4

These tacos are crunchy, a little spicy and a little zingy! This recipe is also a budget-friendly way of eating healthily! You can use shop-bought tacos to save time, although I prefer to make my own. If you can't find it anywhere else, masa harina flour is available online at www.picadomexican.com.

• • • • • • • • • • • • •

2 hake fillets

1 portion tomato salsa
(see p. 95)

FOR THE TACO SHELLS (MAKES 8):

250g masa harina flour,
plus extra for dusting

125g water

Rapeseed oil

FOR THE SPICE MIX:

1 teaspoon sea salt

1 teaspoon caster sugar

1 teaspoon ground cumin

1 teaspoon ground coriander

½ teaspoon chilli powder

½ teaspoon oregano

½ teaspoon ground black
pepper

½ teaspoon paprika

2 tablespoons rapeseed oil

FOR THE GUACAMOLE:

1 avocado, ripe and roughly
chopped

1 clove of garlic, minced

Juice of ½ lime

A small handful of fresh
coriander, chopped

Red chilli, deseeded and
chopped finely

A pinch of sea salt flakes

Place the flour into a bowl and add the water. Mix until thoroughly combined and leave to sit for at least 30 minutes as this will help prevent the tacos from crumbling later.

Preheat the oven to 180°C/fan 160°C/gas mark 4.

Place two sheets of baking paper on your work surface and lightly dust with a little more flour. Take a piece of the dough, about the size of a golf ball, and roll into a ball. Place on one sheet of the floured paper and put the other sheet on top of it. Roll it out into a disk shape, then lightly brush with rapeseed oil. Place the tacos in an upside-down muffin tin to create a cup shape and bake for 15 minutes or until crispy.

Combine all the ingredients for the tomato salsa (see p. 95) in a bowl at least 10 minutes before serving.

For the guacamole, mash all the ingredients together in a bowl until all are combined. Taste and adjust the seasoning if necessary.

Mix together all the ingredients for the spice mix and then rub onto the skinless side of the fish.

Heat a frying pan until good and hot and place the fish spice-side down on the pan. Fry for a couple of minutes to cook the spices, then turn. Fry for another minute or two (depending on the thickness of your fish) and turn the pan off to allow the fish to rest in the pan for a moment or two.

Break the fish up gently, place in the room-temperature taco cups, and top with the salsa and some guacamole.

CASUAL SUPPERS FOR FRIENDS

· · · · · · · · · · · · · · · ·

THE IDEA BEHIND THIS CHAPTER IS TO GIVE YOU SOME SUGGESTIONS FOR IMPROMPTU GATHERINGS. LAST-MINUTE INVITATIONS AFTER WORK, AFTERNOON COFFEE THAT TURNED INTO A DINNER ... THOSE TIMES WHEN YOU ARE NOT PREPARED FOR ENTERTAINING BUT IT JUST HAPPENED. AFTER MY DAUGHTER WAS BORN, I SOMETIMES FOUND IT HARD BEING ON MY OWN EVERY DAY WITH HER, SO IT WAS FUN TO HAVE FRIENDS WITH YOUNG CHILDREN OVER FOR THE AFTERNOON. THESE MINI GATHERINGS OFTEN TURNED INTO DINNER AS THE 'WITCHING HOUR' APPROACHED! THESE RECIPES ARE DESIGNED IN SUCH A WAY THAT THERE'S HOPEFULLY NO NEED TO GO TO THE SHOPS — MOST OF THE INGREDIENTS SHOULD BE IN YOUR STORE CUPBOARD OR FREEZER.

SAFFRON, PRAWN + FENNEL RISOTTO

SERVES 4

What I love about this recipe is the fact that you can feed quite a few from one pan and there's not much washing up. Obviously fresh, plump prawns are nicer, but if you find yourself making this last minute, simply throw a few frozen prawns into the pan about 5 minutes before the end. You can omit the bulb of fennel and add another teaspoon of fennel seeds instead, and you can also use dried thyme if you don't have fresh.

• • • • • • • • • • • • • •

Olive oil

2 shallots, finely chopped

Salt

2 cloves of garlic, finely chopped

1 bulb of fennel, chopped, fronds reserved for serving

1 teaspoon fennel seeds, ground in a pestle and mortar

2 sprigs of thyme

100ml dry white wine

A large knob of butter

200g Arborio Risotto rice

A few saffron strands, immersed in 4 tablespoons of boiling water

750ml chicken or vegetable stock

12 plump Dublin Bay prawns (approx.)

Juice of ½ lemon

100g Parmesan cheese, grated

2 sprigs of flat-leaf parsley, finely chopped

Put a glug of olive oil into a large frying pan over a medium heat and gently sweat the shallots with a little salt until softened.

When the shallots are almost ready, add the garlic, fennel bulb and seeds, and thyme leaves and stir for a couple of minutes.

Deglaze the pan with the white wine, then add the butter after the liquid has boiled away.

Add the rice to the pan, stirring to make sure it is coated in the oil – add a little more oil if necessary.

Strain the saffron through a small sieve, reserving the water and discarding the saffron. Add the water from the saffron to the rice and cook until it is absorbed. Then start to add the stock, a ladleful at a time, stirring all the time. You should allow each ladleful to be absorbed by the rice before adding the next. It should take 20–25 minutes for all the liquid to be absorbed.

In the meantime, place the prawns in a pot and cover with cold water. Bring to the boil, then remove to a colander immediately. The prawns should have just turned opaque with a pinkish colour. Be careful not to overcook.

When all the stock has been absorbed by the rice, add lemon juice to taste, then add the prawns and stir the Parmesan cheese through the risotto. Serve with a little parsley and the reserved fennel fronds on top.

TOAD IN THE HOLE WITH ONION + MUSHROOM GRAVY

SERVES 4

I always keep a few sausages in the fridge or freezer. My butcher in Termonfeckin makes great sausages and they are a brilliant stand-by ingredient. This one is particularly popular with visiting kids.

• • • • • • • • • • • •

Vegetable or rapeseed oil
6–8 large sausages

FOR THE BATTER:
250ml milk
115g plain flour
A pinch of salt
2 eggs

FOR THE GRAVY:
A knob of butter
1 small onion, finely diced
1 teaspoon tomato purée
3–4 mushrooms, sliced
1 tablespoon flour
250ml beef stock
1 teaspoon redcurrant jelly

Preheat the oven to 200°C/fan 180°C/gas mark 6.

Mix the ingredients for the batter together in a jug and set aside.

Put a glug of oil in a roasting dish and place in the oven until very hot. Add the sausages to the hot oil and return to the oven. Cook for about 5 minutes or until turning golden.

Add the batter to the hot dish, being careful as it will spit a little. Return to the oven for about 20 minutes or until the batter has cooked and is golden brown. While it is cooking, make the gravy.

Melt the butter in a saucepan over a medium heat and add the onion. Sauté gently until soft, then add the tomato purée and mushrooms. Cook for a minute or so, then add the flour. Continue cooking for about 3 minutes, stirring.

Add the beef stock and keep on a low simmer until thickened. Stir in the redcurrant jelly and check for seasoning.

Serve the toad in the hole with a little of the gravy over the top – you should have enough left over to bring an extra jug of gravy to the table.

STIR-FRIED ASIAN MINCE
IN LETTUCE CUPS

SERVES 4

This is one of my husband's favourite quick dishes. Feel free to play around with the spices, and pork mince works well here or, if you are on a health kick, turkey mince lends itself well to this recipe too. The main thing to remember is to cook everything hot and fast, stirring regularly, as it can become dry very quickly.

• • • • • • • • • • • •

1 tablespoon rapeseed oil

500g beef mince (lean if possible)

3 cloves of garlic, thinly sliced

1 teaspoon grated fresh ginger

1 teaspoon dried chilli flakes

1 teaspoon ground cumin

2 tablespoons nam pla
(Thai fish sauce)

2 spring onions, chopped

1 teaspoon toasted sesame oil

½ teaspoon runny honey

Juice of ½ lime

2 heads of little gem lettuce,
leaves removed and washed

FOR THE GARNISH:

2 tablespoons cashew nuts,
roughly chopped

A handful of coriander leaves,
chopped

1 red chilli, sliced thinly on the
diagonal

½ lime, cut into 4 wedges

Heat the rapeseed oil in a wok. When sizzling, add the mince and stir-fry until it begins to brown. Add the garlic, ginger, dried chilli and cumin. It's good to toast the spices a little before adding the wet ingredients, as the spices can be a bit chalky otherwise.

Finally, add the fish sauce, spring onions, sesame oil, honey and lime juice, and stir-fry until they are bubbling and the beef is nicely browned.

Place the cashew nuts on a dry pan and toast until golden brown.

To serve, put a large tablespoonful of the mince mixture into each little gem leaf and serve topped with fresh coriander, a little chilli, a sprinkling of toasted nuts and a wedge of lime on the side.

SMOKEY BEAN STEW

SERVES 4

I always have a few tins of mixed beans and tinned tomatoes in my store cupboard, which makes it very easy to pull this together at the last minute. Don't worry if you don't have fresh rosemary, a teaspoon of herbes de Provence or mixed herbs goes well in here too. For a really handy cheat, you can buy packs of bacon lardons, freeze them and pop them into the oil from frozen. Also very handy for serving with this is part-baked baguette, which I always have in the freezer – it can be baked from frozen.

• • • • • • • • • • • • • •

Rapeseed oil

1 onion, chopped

Salt

1 clove of garlic, finely chopped

1 sprig of rosemary, chopped

6 rashers of streaky bacon, chopped, or 100g bacon lardons

100ml chicken or vegetable stock

1 x 400g tin of chopped tomatoes

2 x 400g tins of mixed beans

A little Parmesan cheese, grated

Pour some oil into a saucepan and add the onion with a pinch of salt and sweat gently until softened, then add the garlic, rosemary and bacon.

When the bacon is browned, add the stock, the tomatoes and beans.

Simmer for 30–40 minutes, making sure it doesn't dry out. Add a little water if necessary and stir regularly.

Top with the grated Parmesan cheese when serving. This is delicious served with chunks of fresh crusty bread.

NO-HASSLE SMOKED SALMON PASTA

SERVES 4

This one-pan meal really is for those days when you have no time and no inclination (or are just feeling lazy!) but are in need of sustenance. It is light but filling, and tasty and ideal for eating on the couch with your feet up.

• • • • • • • • • • • • •

200g penne or tagliatelle pasta

150ml crème fraîche

200g smoked salmon

150g peas (fresh or frozen) or asparagus

A squeeze of lemon juice

Salt and pepper

Boil the pasta according to the pack instructions, keeping a ladleful of cooking water to one side before you drain the water. If using asparagus add it to the pasta for the last 2–3 minutes of cooking time.

Return the pasta to the still-warm cooking pot and add the crème fraîche, smoked salmon and peas or asparagus with the cooking liquid. Turn the heat on gently and stir to ensure all the ingredients are mixed through and fully heated.

Add a good squeeze of lemon juice and salt and pepper to taste.

CATERING
FOR A CROWD

· ·

I HAVE INCLUDED A SELECTION HERE OF NIBBLES, MAINS AND SIDES, AS YOU WILL NEED ALL OF THESE WHEN CATERING FOR A CROWD. I HAVE ALSO INCLUDED MY TOP TEN TIPS FOR CATERING FOR A LARGE EVENT, WHICH SHOULD HELP MAKE THE DAY RUN SMOOTHLY AND, HOPEFULLY, STRESS-FREE.

MY TOP TEN TIPS FOR CATERING FOR AN EVENT

· · · · · · · · · · ·

- Place nibbles on big platters in other areas around the house such as the sitting room, hall and so on, to keep people out from under your feet while you get everything ready. Make sure you leave small napkins with the nibbles.

- If you are catering for a communion/confirmation/wedding, people are usually dying for a cup of tea or coffee after a long service at church, so set up a tea and coffee area away from the kitchen. Have cups, teaspoons, milk and sugar ready the day before. If you are having a big crowd, you may want to consider borrowing a water boiler.

- Use disposable roasting dishes and trays wherever possible to reduce the clean-up, and make sure the dishwasher (if you have one) is empty beforehand.

- There are plenty of pretty disposable plates, cups and napkins available nowadays. If you don't want to use these for everybody, then at least use them for the children.

- A relaxed host will create a much more relaxed atmosphere, so accept help from others, whether it is bringing some food on the day or serving tea and coffee to elderly relatives during the event.

- Get organised in advance – all the recipes here can be made beforehand and frozen or refrigerated. Having as much done as possible in advance will allow you to enjoy the day.

- Make a list in advance of all the jobs you need to do, e.g. when things need to be reheated and for how long, so that you don't forget anything when people are trying to have a chat with you. I often write it on a post-it note and stick it to the inside of a cupboard door.

- Set your buffet table beforehand with all the necessaries.

- If you have a lot of young children at the event, make up little goodie bags with a few crayons and mini colouring books and toys to keep the children occupied whilst the adults are eating.

- Have lots of freezer bags ready for leftovers.

GUINNESS BROWN BREAD

MAKES 1 LOAF

This is one of the most popular breads we make at the cookery school. It is great served with a seafood starter and smoked fish as it has a lovely yeasty but sweet taste. It is incredibly easy to make and keeps well for two to three days. It can also be frozen.

• • • • • • • • • • • • •

50g butter, plus extra for greasing

1 tablespoon honey

450g wholemeal flour

2 tablespoons oatmeal

4 tablespoons light-brown sugar

A large handful of walnuts, chopped (optional)

2 level teaspoons bicarbonate of soda (bread soda)

400ml Guinness

Preheat the oven to 200°C/fan 180°C/gas mark 6.

Grease a 900g/2lb loaf tin with a small amount of melted butter and line the bottom with parchment paper.

Put the butter and honey in a saucepan and melt over a low heat.

Meanwhile, put the wholemeal flour, oatmeal, sugar and chopped walnuts (if using) into a bowl.

Sieve in the bicarbonate of soda and mix well.

Add the Guinness to the melted butter and honey and stir together. Add this liquid to the dry ingredients and mix gently to form a wet dough.

Transfer the mixture to the prepared tin and bake for about 40–50 minutes until risen – when tapped underneath it should have a hollow sound.

Wrap in a clean tea towel and allow to cool before slicing.

CITRUS, FENNEL + PINK PEPPERCORN MARINATED SALMON

SERVES 8–10

This is a great starter to feed a crowd: fantastic salmon at a purse-friendly price! Traditional smoked salmon is always a popular starter, so why not try this lovely, light alternative? A full side of smoked salmon costs in and around €45 to buy, whereas a side of fresh salmon is approximately €20.

Juice of 1 lemon

Juice of 2 limes

100ml olive oil

2 tablespoons fennel fronds (or dill), chopped, plus a little extra to garnish

1 tablespoon pink peppercorns, crushed

1 shallot, finely chopped

400g salmon fillet, very finely sliced

Sea salt

½ green pepper, very finely chopped

Mix the lemon and lime juices with the olive oil. Add the chopped fennel, pink peppercorns and shallot.

Spread the mixture out on a platter, holding a couple of tablespoons back. Place the salmon slices on top, sprinkle with a little sea salt and pour the remaining mixture over the salmon, ensuring any of the protruding pieces have some of the citrus juice over them as this is essentially what cooks it. Marinate for 15–30 minutes.

To serve, sprinkle with the green pepper and fennel on top. This is lovely with the Guinness Brown Bread (see p. 149).

GOAT'S CHEESE TARTLETS WITH BASIL OR WILD GARLIC PESTO

MAKES 12 LARGE OR 18 MINI

These tartlets can be made the day before and kept in the fridge or freezer. Simply reheat at 200°C/fan 180°C/gas mark 6 for 3–4 minutes from the fridge or for 6–7 minutes from frozen, before topping with a little of the pesto. They are ideal nibbles for occasions that involve standing around! You can also make a larger tart as a main course – very handy if you have a vegetarian guest! Simply cut out a rectangular shape of pastry and make an incision all the way around about a centimetre in from the edge. Place the toppings in the middle and brush the outer pastry with egg wash before baking as usual.

• • • • • • • • • • • • •

FOR THE TARTLETS:

Olive oil

1 sheet of shop-bought, ready-rolled puff pastry

A handful of cherry tomatoes, sliced in half

½ red onion, thinly sliced

1 log of goat's cheese

FOR THE PESTO:

A large handful of fresh basil or wild garlic

2 cloves of garlic (not needed if you are using wild garlic)

3–4 tablespoons extra virgin olive oil

3–4 tablespoons pinenuts (for basil) or walnuts (for wild garlic), toasted

30g Parmesan cheese, grated

Salt and black pepper

Preheat the oven to 180°C/fan 160°C/gas mark 4.

Grease a 12-hole muffin or 18-hole mini-muffin tin with a tiny bit of oil (I find a silicon brush handy for this job). Cut the puff pastry into circles and place into the individual bun moulds in the tin.

Place half a tomato, a little onion and a thin slice of goat's cheese into each pastry round.

Place in the oven and bake for approximately 20–25 minutes, or until golden brown and puffed up.

To make the pesto, place the basil/wild garlic in a food processor and pulse briefly. Add the garlic (if using), 3 tablespoons of olive oil and pinenuts/walnuts, and pulse again. If necessary add the last tablespoon of oil and pulse again – you don't want the pesto too dry but you also don't want it too liquid or it will run off the top of the tartlets.

Remove to a bowl and fold in the grated Parmesan. Check for flavour and add seasoning if necessary.

Put a little pesto on top of each tart and serve warm.

FRAGRANT + CREAMY CHICKEN CURRY

SERVES 8-10

20 chicken thighs, boned and skinned (ask your butcher to do this for you)

1 teaspoon turmeric, ground

1 teaspoon cumin, ground

1 teaspoon garam masala

A pinch of dried chilli flakes (optional)

Groundnut oil

1 onion, sliced

A pinch of salt

2 cloves of garlic, chopped

A thumb-sized piece of fresh ginger, grated

1 teaspoon tomato purée

750ml chicken stock

100ml pouring cream

400g mixed vegetables (such as baby corn, sugar snaps, mangetout, green beans, red pepper) blanched or steamed

TARA'S TIP:

CHOOSE HOW SPICY YOU WANT THIS CURRY TO BE – ADD EXTRA CHILLI FLAKES TO THE MARINADE AND SCATTER A CHOPPED RED CHILLI OR TWO OVER AT THE END FOR AN EXTRA KICK!

This chicken curry is a winner with both children and elderly relatives. It is flavoursome without being too spicy. It can be made ahead of time and chilled or frozen until you are ready to serve it. If you are making it ahead of time and want to add the vegetables, it is best to steam or blanch them and mix them through just before serving, as this will keep them crisp and help them maintain their colour.

Slice the chicken into bite-sized pieces.

In a large bowl, mix the spices with a couple of tablespoons of water to make a paste and coat the chicken with it. Cover and refrigerate for at least an hour.

Heat some oil in a pan until quite hot and add the chicken pieces to brown. Remove to a bowl and set aside.

Add the onion and a pinch of salt to the pan with a little more oil if necessary. Sweat until softened. Add the garlic and ginger for the last few minutes of sweating.

Add the tomato purée and cook for a minute or two. Return the chicken to the pot and cover with the stock and the cream. Simmer for about 25 minutes on a low heat or until the chicken is cooked through and the sauce has thickened.

Just before serving, add the vegetables. This is lovely with the sticky basmati rice on page 167 or the chilli and coriander naan bread on page 165.

MELTING SLOW-ROASTED SHOULDER OF PULLED LAMB

SERVES 8

Catering for a crowd is always going to have some level of stress attached to it, but this lamb is fantastic in that it feeds eight people from one large pot which disappears into the oven for 4 hours, while you get on with the rest of your preparations. It will also rest quite nicely for a couple of hours in a warm place if your guests are late.

• • • • • • • • • • • • • • •

1 shoulder of lamb

Salt and pepper

Rapeseed oil

1 large carrot, cut into chunks

1 large onion, quartered

1 stick of celery, cut into chunks

Soy sauce

Worcestershire sauce

Zest of 1 lemon

1 large sprig of mint, chopped

Preheat the oven to 150°C/fan 130°C/gas mark 2.

Trim any heavy, excess fat from the shoulder and season the lamb.

Add some oil to a heavy-bottomed, ovenproof pot on the hob and heat until very hot. Place the lamb fat-side down in the oil to sear it until golden brown. Turn and brown on all sides. Remove to a plate.

Add some more oil to the pot and add the carrot, onion and celery. When softened a little, place the lamb on the vegetables and sprinkle with 5–6 drops each of soy sauce and Worcestershire sauce.

Cover with either a lid or some tinfoil. Place in the oven for 4 hours. When done, remove the lamb to a warmed dish to rest (for at least 30 minutes) and discard the vegetables (my dog loves the carrot!).

When it's rested, pull the lamb apart with two forks or with your hands (wearing disposable gloves). The meat should just fall off the bone.

Place on a serving platter. Sprinkle with the lemon zest and mint and serve with raita (see p. 58). This is lovely with roast potatoes, gravy and some seasonal vegetables (without the raita, mint and lemon) in winter, or with new potatoes and a green salad in summer.

155

SLOW-BRAISED BEEF CHEEKS

SERVES 6-8

If you like a rich beef stew, you'll love this. Beef cheeks are not a commonly used part of the cow and will probably need to be ordered in advance from your butcher, but when they are cooked for a long time they are really flavourful and tender. The great thing about these is you can put them on to cook and then forget about them while you are doing anything else you need to do to get ready.

• • • • • • • • • • • • • • • •

2 large beef cheeks

2 carrots, cut into chunks

2 onions, quartered

2 sticks of celery, cut into chunks

2 cloves of garlic, sliced

1 bouquet garni

500ml beef stock

500ml red wine

A few black peppercorns

2 tablespoons rapeseed oil

Salt

1 tablespoon tomato purée

FOR THE GARNISH:

1 small red onion

Juice of ½ lemon

3 sprigs of parsley, finely chopped

Preheat the oven to 170°C/fan 150°C/gas mark 3.

Place the beef cheeks in a bowl and cover with vegetables, bouquet garni, stock, red wine and peppercorns. Cover with cling film and place in the fridge overnight.

When you are ready to cook the beef, remove the meat and vegetables from the rest of the ingredients (reserving the liquid and bouquet garni) to a plate and dry off with kitchen paper.

Heat the oil over a fairly high heat in a large casserole dish or any large ovenproof pot that you have and add the meat. Brown on both sides and then remove to a plate.

Reduce the heat and add the vegetables and a pinch of salt. Cover and cook for 5–10 minutes or until the vegetables have softened.

Stir the tomato purée into the casserole and cook for a minute or two, then put the beef back into the casserole and add the reserved liquid and the bouquet garni.

Cover the dish and place it in the oven for 4 hours or until the meat is so tender it is falling apart.

Just before the meat is cooked, make the garnish. Thinly slice the onion, pour the lemon juice over it and add the parsley.

When the meat is ready, set a large colander or sieve over a bowl or jug and strain the meat juices into it. Put the juice into a saucepan and bring to the boil. Allow to boil vigorously for at least 10 minutes (longer if possible), until the sauce has reduced by half and has become much thicker.

While the sauce is reducing, discard the vegetables and pull the meat apart using two forks, or do this with your hands using disposable gloves.

Serve a quarter of a beef cheek to each person, pour some of the reduced braising liquid over the meat and top with some of the garnish. Serve with mashed potatoes, a green salad and French dressing (see p. 56), or steamed greens such as broccoli or green beans.

TARA'S TIP:
I ALWAYS START MY GRAVY BEFORE I PUT MY MEAT IN THE OVEN, THEN LET IT SIMMER ON A VERY LOW HEAT WHILE THE MEAT COOKS, AS IT GIVES THE GRAVY A MUCH RICHER FLAVOUR.

MULLED CIDER MARINATED LOIN OF PORK WITH CHESTNUT STUFFING + CIDER GRAVY

SERVES 6-8

This recipe is one I often do at my Christmas cookery classes and it's a great excuse to have some mulled cider on the go!

• • • • • • • • • • • • • • •

1 boned loin of pork (about 1½ kg)
Sea salt
1 carrot, skin on, quartered
1 onion, skin on, quartered
1 stick of celery, roughly chopped
Worcestershire sauce
Soy sauce

FOR THE MARINADE:
Freshly grated nutmeg
250ml cider
1 stick cinnamon
A pinch of ground ginger
A pinch of mixed spice
3 cloves
2 star anise
Zest of ½ orange

FOR THE STUFFING:
75g butter
1 small onion, finely diced
250g breadcrumbs
150g chestnuts (the vacuum-packed ones are fine), chopped
2 tablespoons of sweetened chestnut purée (from a can)
Freshly grated nutmeg
A small bunch of parsley, chopped
Zest of 1 lemon
Salt and pepper

Firstly, make the marinade. Take a nutmeg seed and grate it four or five times with the accompanying grater into a saucepan. Add all the other ingredients and heat. Do not boil but keep warm for at least five minutes to allow the flavours to infuse. Remove from the heat and allow to cool.

To prepare the pork, score the skin fairly deeply without cutting the flesh at ½cm intervals. (You can ask your butcher to do this for you.) Place the pork into a shallow dish and pour the marinade on top. Rub it into the pork to ensure it is coated. Cover and leave to marinate in the fridge for at least 4 hours, but overnight is best.

Make the stuffing by melting the butter in a saucepan and gently frying the onion. When the onion has softened but is not too coloured, add the breadcrumbs and stir well to coat in the butter. Add the chopped chestnuts and chestnut purée and combine well. Finally, add a few gratings of nutmeg, the parsley and the lemon zest. Season to taste. Remove from the heat and allow to cool.

Preheat the oven to 220°C/fan 200°C/gas mark 6.

When you are ready to cook the pork, remove it from the marinade and pat it dry with some kitchen paper. Strain the marinade into a jug and reserve the liquid to use for the gravy.

Lay the pork out skin-side down on a board and place the chestnut stuffing in the hollow where the bone would have been. Roll up tightly and tie with cook's string at 1cm

25g butter

25g plain flour

100ml reserved marinade (add some extra cider if you don't have 100ml left)

150ml chicken stock

1 teaspoon soy sauce

intervals. It is important to do this thoroughly or the stuffing may fall out during the cooking. Rub some sea salt into the skin and make sure it is pushed into the scored fat.

Place the carrot, onion and celery in a roasting dish and lay the pork on top. Douse the pork with the Worcestershire sauce and soy sauce and rub them in well. Place a small amount of water into the roasting dish (about 1cm in depth). Cover with tinfoil.

Place in the oven for 30 minutes. After this time, reduce the temperature to 180°C/fan 160°C/gas mark 4. Remove the tinfoil and cook for a further 2 hours. To check if the pork is cooked insert a skewer into the middle. The skewer should feel too hot to place against your lip when the meat is cooked through. Remove the pork from the dish, reserving the cooking juices but discarding the rest, and allow to rest on a plate in a warm place for at least 30 minutes.

While the pork is roasting, make your gravy. Melt the butter in a saucepan over a medium heat, add the flour and combine to make a roux. Cook for about 5 minutes (a good way to know the flour is cooked is by smelling some of the mixture – it should smell like baked biscuits or pastry). Add the reserved marinade and chicken stock. Bring the gravy to the boil, then add the soy sauce. Don't panic if it looks lumpy as boiling and whisking energetically at the same time will get rid of any lumps. Once it is smooth, bring it back to a gentle simmer.

When the pork is cooked, add the strained juices to the gravy. Simmer until the gravy has thickened and the flavours have intensified sufficiently.

Carve the pork and serve with the gravy. This is lovely with my rustic herby roast potatoes (see p. 166).

LAMB TAGINE WITH PRESERVED LEMONS

SERVES 6

One of the most popular dishes from all our classes, this Moroccan-style lamb tagine is a fantastic way of feeding a crowd as you can do all the work the day before and simply reheat on the day of your party. It's much easier if you ask your butcher to bone the meat for you.

● • ● • ● • ● • ● • ● • ● • ● • ●

1.5kg shoulder of lamb, boned, trimmed and cut it into 2cm dices

Rapeseed oil

2 onions, chopped

2 cloves of garlic, minced or finely chopped

2 x 400g tins of chopped tomatoes

500ml lamb stock

3 tablespoons honey

1 aubergine, chopped into cubes

A handful of dried apricots, chopped

½ preserved lemon, pips removed, quartered

A large handful of flaked almonds, toasted

A bunch of fresh coriander, chopped

FOR THE MARINADE:

2 tablespoons ground cinnamon

1½ tablespoons ground ginger

1 teaspoon ground cumin

1½ tablespoons paprika

1 teaspoon cayenne

2 teaspoons ground black pepper

1 teaspoon ras el hanout

Mix the marinade ingredients with 5 tablespoons of water in a large bowl. Add the lamb and ensure it is well coated. Cover and leave for 24 hours if possible.

Add a good glug of oil to a large casserole dish and heat on the hob over a high heat.

Brown the lamb in batches, ensuring you keep the dish hot. When all the lamb is cooked, set aside.

Reduce the heat and add more oil. Add the onions and sweat for 5 minutes, then add the garlic and stir for 1–2 minutes.

Return the lamb to the pot and add the tomatoes, stock and honey.

Bring to the boil, cover and then place in the oven. Stir after 1½ hours and add the aubergine, apricots and preserved lemon.

Return to the oven for 1 hour.

When serving, sprinkle with the almonds and coriander. I love this served with the tabbouleh on page 184. It can also be served with some plain couscous and the radish, orange and olive salad on page 168.

SIDES

CHILLI + CORIANDER NAAN BREAD

SERVES 8

I often make the dough for this a day in advance and keep it in the fridge, or you can make it further in advance and freeze it. Just make sure you give it at least 6 hours to defrost.

• • • • • • • • • • •

1 egg

250ml milk

450g plain flour

2 teaspoons sugar

1 teaspoon salt

1 teaspoon baking powder

2 tablespoons sunflower oil

1 fresh red chilli, chopped

A handful of fresh coriander leaves, chopped

A knob of butter, melted

A few pinches of sea salt

Whisk the egg into the milk.

Sieve the flour, sugar, salt and baking powder onto your work surface. Make a well in the centre and start to add the milk mixture. Bring the dough together by mixing all the ingredients and knead for 3–4 minutes.

Place the dough in a bowl coated with the oil and cover with cling film. Leave to rest for 1 hour at room temperature.

When ready to cook the naan, divide the dough into golfball-sized amounts. Roll into a ball in your hand, then flatten out by pulling and turning it with your hands until it is quite thin.

Heat a griddle pan until hot and place the naans on it.

Press the chilli and coriander onto the surface of each naan and turn over when the bottom is well cooked. When cooked, there should be nice griddle marks and a golden-brown crust.

While they are still in the pan brush the naans with the melted butter and top with a little sea salt.

RUSTIC HERBY ROAST POTATOES

SERVES 8-10

These potatoes are great for cooking for a crowd as they are quick and fuss free. You can prepare them the day before and leave them in the fridge, covered. Then, when your guests are there, pop them in the oven. If you have a nice roasting dish, simply serve them in it. The crispy, sticky bits will only add to their appeal!

• • • • • • • • • • • • •

6 tablespoons olive oil

1kg rooster potatoes, scrubbed and cubed with skin on

A selection of woody herbs such as rosemary, thyme and sage

1 bulb of garlic broken into cloves, peeled but left whole

Salt and pepper

Preheat the oven to 200°C/fan 180°C /gas mark 6.

Pour the oil into a roasting dish and place in the oven. When you are sure the oil is very hot, remove the dish from the oven and place the potatoes in the oil, making sure to coat them thoroughly. Add the herbs and garlic and sprinkle with salt and pepper.

Roast for about 30 minutes or until golden brown and crisp on the outside.

STICKY BASMATI RICE

SERVES 4

250g basmati rice
375ml water
Salt

This sticky rice is perfect for soaking up all the lovely sauce from a curry or with sticky chicken drumsticks.

• ● • ● • ● • ● • ● • ● • ●

Place the rice in the pot with the water, making sure it is at least half an inch above the height of the rice – add more water if necessary. Add a pinch of salt and boil for 10 minutes.

When all of the water is absorbed, turn the heat off and cover but DO NOT STIR! Leave to steam for at least 10 minutes.

Fluff up with a fork before serving.

RADISH, ORANGE AND OLIVE SALAD

This salad is a fantastic foil to the warm spice of the lamb tagine. Try to use the best olives you can find. I love to use the Kalamata variety and stone them myself, as I think they have a superior flavour.

• • • • • • • • • • • •

SERVES 6

2 large oranges

15 radishes, thinly sliced

10 black olives, sliced in half

2 tablespoons extra virgin olive oil

1 clove of garlic, minced

Salt and pepper

Segment the oranges, making sure you save any juice.

Layer up slices of the radish, orange segments and olive halves on a nice wide shallow platter.

Place the olive oil, garlic, salt and pepper and any juice from the orange in a jar and shake. Drizzle over the salad just before serving.

BARBECUE

A NOTE ABOUT BARBECUING: THE BEST WAY TO DO IT IS TO LIGHT THE BARBECUE IN ADVANCE OF COOKING. INITIALLY IT NEEDS TO BE HOTTER THAN YOU WOULD LIKE TO COOK, AS THIS WILL STERILISE THE GRILL AND GET THE HEAT GOING. WHEN IT IS REALLY GOOD AND HOT (ABOUT 10 MINUTES FOR A GAS BARBECUE AND 30 MINUTES FOR A CHARCOAL ONE), USE A WIRE BRUSH OR SCRAPER TO CLEAN THE RACK. REDUCE THE TEMPERATURE TO ABOUT 200°C. IF YOU ARE USING A GAS BARBECUE THIS IS EASY; FOR A COAL BARBECUE, AS A RULE OF THUMB, YOU SHOULD ONLY BE ABLE TO HOVER YOUR HAND OVER THE SURFACE FOR ABOUT 5 SECONDS. AVOID COOKING ON DIRECT FLAME AS THIS WILL BURN THE OUTSIDE WHILE LEAVING THE MIDDLE RAW. IT IS A GOOD IDEA TO KEEP A SILICONE BRUSH AND A LITTLE JUG OF A HIGH-BURNING-POINT OIL, SUCH AS GROUNDNUT, SUNFLOWER OR RAPESEED, NEXT TO THE BARBECUE TO KEEP EVERYTHING WELL OILED. WHILE BARBECUING, TRY NOT TO CONSTANTLY MOVE THE FOOD AROUND — ALLOW IT TO SIT AND SEAR!

GRIDDLED PRAWN SKEWERS WITH COURGETTE, WILD RICE + CHILLI SALAD

SERVES 4

This is a nice simple summery lunch or suppertime dish. It really is perfect for the barbecue and is best enjoyed al fresco with a chilled glass of white wine. A crisp Sauvignon Blanc would be good, or maybe even a Riesling or Gewürztraminer. You can also cook this dish on a griddle pan if you don't have a barbecue to hand, or if it's raining!

• • • • • • • • • • • • • • •

16 prawns (plump and fresh – Dublin Bay are by far the best for this)

Extra virgin olive oil

1 clove of garlic, chopped

1 red chilli, sliced

Zest and juice of 1 lemon

1 courgette, sliced thinly lengthways

Sea salt flakes

A handful of flaked almonds

100g wild rice, boiled and still warm

100g feta or goat's cheese, crumbled

A small bunch of fresh mint, chopped

Thread the prawns onto a skewer and place in a shallow bowl. Drizzle with some oil, then sprinkle with half of the garlic and chilli (check your chilli for heat!) and the lemon zest.

With the barbecue on a medium heat, place the skewers on it, turning occasionally until the prawns are opaque and pink. Try not to overcook them. A little of the coating will fall off, but some will stay nice and charred. Depending on the size of the prawns, cooking shouldn't take longer than 5–7 minutes.

In the meantime, drizzle the courgette with a little oil and season with some sea salt flakes. Place these directly on the barbecue too. Turn after 3 minutes and cook until softened and charred a little.

Toast the almonds on a dry pan until they turn golden.

In a bowl, place the still-warm rice with the courgette, cheese and lemon juice, then add a little olive oil and salt. Add the remainder of the garlic and chilli. Taste and adjust the seasoning if necessary. Once you are happy with this, top with the mint and toasted flaked almonds. Serve alongside the prawns.

EASY FRAGRANT BUTTERFLIED LEG OF LAMB WITH RAITA + POMEGRANATE SEEDS

SERVES 8-10

If you have already marinated the meat, but the weather lets you down on the day, you can cook this in the oven instead. Just preheat the oven to 180°C/fan 160°C /gas mark 4 and cook as instructed.

• • • • • • • • • • • •

1 butterflied leg of lamb

A portion of raita (see p. 58)

A bunch of fresh mint

A handful of pomegranate seeds

FOR THE MARINADE:

2 teaspoons coriander seeds

2 teaspoons fennel seeds

2 teaspoons cumin seeds

2 tablespoons cardamom pods

1 teaspoon cayenne pepper

100ml olive oil (bog standard is fine for this)

50ml soy sauce

Zest of 1 orange

5 cloves of garlic, roughly chopped

Place the coriander seeds in a dry pan and gently toast for a few seconds, then add the fennel and cumin seeds and continue to toast for 2–3 minutes or until they release their aroma.

Place all the seeds and the cardamom pods in a pestle and mortar and grind. As this is a rustic dish, leave the cardamom pods, which won't break down fully, in the mix as they are easily removable later and give a fantastic flavour.

Mix all the marinade ingredients together and pour over the lamb. Leave in the fridge overnight if possible but give it at least 6 hours to infuse.

Take the lamb out of the fridge an hour before cooking. Remove from the marinade, but reserve the liquid for later. Heat the barbecue to a high heat (smoking) and place the lamb on. The idea is to char the outside.

Reduce the temperature of the barbecue (if using solid fuel remove the meat and allow the fuel to cool for a few minutes, letting the flames die down), then continue to cook, basting with the reserved marinade, for about 20–30 minutes, or until cooked to your liking.

Allow to rest for at least 10 minutes before carving.

While you are waiting, make the raita.

Before carving the meat remove any visible cardamom pods. Arrange the slices of meat on a platter and scatter with the mint leaves and pomegranate seeds. Serve the raita on the side or drizzle over the lamb. This is lovely served with the tabbouleh on page 184, the barbecued vegetables on page 182 or the superfood salad from page 185.

SPATCHCOCK CHICKEN

SERVES 4

A spatchcocked chicken is one that has had the backbone and sometimes the sternum removed so it can be flattened for cooking. You can do this yourself, or ask your butcher to do it for you. This is a very handy way to cook chicken on a barbecue or a griddle pan, but it can also be done in the oven – just leave out the skewers and cook for half an hour at a heat of 200°C/fan 180°C/gas mark 6. It's a great way to serve a whole chicken quickly as it needs a lot less time to cook when it is flattened out. Metal skewers are useful here as they conduct the heat and help the chicken cook from the centre out, which can prevent the outside from becoming overcooked.

• • • • • • • • • • •

1.5kg chicken, spatchcocked

2 tablespoons soy sauce

1 tablespoon honey

½ teaspoon paprika

½ teaspoon ground coriander

½ teaspoon fennel seeds, crushed

1 clove of garlic, minced

Place the spatchcocked chicken in a large roasting dish.

Mix together the soy sauce, honey, paprika, ground coriander, fennel and garlic in a bowl. Pour the marinade over the chicken and allow to marinate for at least an hour, but preferably overnight.

When ready to cook push two metal skewers into the chicken. Place the chicken on the barbecue. Keep a close eye on it and turn it regularly to ensure it cooks evenly. Cook for 45–50 minutes in total. You can finish it in the oven at 180°C/fan 160°C/gas mark 4 if it is becoming overly browned on the outside.

Allow the meat to rest for at least 10 minutes before serving. Serve with a big bunch of flat-leaf parsley and the saffron aioli (see p. 128). This is lovely with the rustic herby potatoes on page 166.

STICKY CHARRED PORK FILLET

SERVES 4–6

If you are new to barbecuing this is a great recipe to get you started, as the pork is easy to handle on the barbecue and the marinade is quick to prepare but gives fantastic flavour.

• • • • • • • • • • •

1 whole pork fillet (500g approx.)

FOR THE MARINADE:

1 cup soy sauce

¾ cup brown sugar

¼ cup balsamic vinegar

¼ cup tomato paste

¼ cup orange juice

2 tablespoons grainy mustard

1 teaspoon ground ginger

½ teaspoon ground cinnamon

½ teaspoon hot chilli powder

½ teaspoon cumin powder

Place all the marinade ingredients in a bowl and mix well.

Put the pork in a shallow dish and pour the marinade over, making sure it is well coated. Marinate for 24 hours if possible – the longer the better.

Remove the pork from the dish, reserving the marinade. Place the meat on a hot barbecue and char on all sides.

Reduce the heat of the barbecue (if you have a solid-fuel barbecue, remove the meat and just wait a few minutes to let it cool down). Continue to cook the meat, brushing it with the marinade regularly using a silicone brush until the pork is cooked through. This should take 15–20 minutes. Make sure you don't put any of the marinade on towards the end of the cooking time, as it has raw pork in it and needs to be cooked out.

Allow to rest for 10 minutes on a warmed dish before carving. Serve with any of the sides from this chapter.

SIDES

BARBECUED VEGETABLES

SERVES 4

You can choose any vegetables you fancy – the ones below are simply a combination that I like. When serving these, I like to drizzle them with extra virgin olive oil and lemon juice and sprinkle them with fresh herbs, such as oregano and parsley. The amounts here are generous for four people, but I always find people seem to eat quite a lot when they are outdoors.

• ● • ● • ● • ● • ● • ● • ●

2 heads of baby gem lettuce

1 medium-sized courgette

1 fennel, sliced and blanched

500g potatoes, sliced and blanched

1 red pepper

5 flat-cap mushrooms

Rapeseed oil

Salt and pepper

Arrange all the vegetables on a tray or platter and drizzle with some rapeseed oil. Season to taste.

Place on the barbecue and allow to cook for a few minutes on each side until charred and cooked through.

GRILLED HALLOUMI

Not only does halloumi cheese taste fantastic when barbecued, this is also a great accompaniment for any vegetarian guests who are often not very well catered for at barbecues and are left stuck with just the sides. It also makes a nice starter or nibble to have when your guests arrive.

• • • • • • • • • • • • •

SERVES 2

250g halloumi

Rapeseed oil

A squeeze of lemon juice

Extra virgin olive oil

A few fresh thyme or oregano leaves, chopped

Slice the cheese into ½cm slices lengthways and brush with a little rapeseed oil. With the barbecue on a medium heat, place the halloumi slices directly onto the griddle. Don't worry, this won't melt through the grill, as it is a semi-hard cheese that will hold together when cooked.

Cook until golden brown on the bottom and then turn over.

When the halloumi is cooked, serve warm with a little lemon juice squeezed over it and some extra virgin olive oil drizzled on top. Finally, sprinkle with the thyme or oregano leaves and it's ready to go.

TABBOULEH

SERVES 6

For me the authentic and beautifully nutty bulgur wheat is an essential for tabbouleh, but feel free to use couscous if you are in a hurry. Traditionally tabbouleh has almost more herbs than grain, but here we are serving it with plenty of grain to make it a filling side dish.

• • • • • • • • • • • • • • •

200g bulgur wheat

Chicken stock (enough to more than cover the wheat)

½ red onion, finely chopped

A generous bunch of mint, roughly chopped

A generous bunch of coriander, roughly chopped

A generous bunch of flat-leaf parsley, roughly chopped

Lemon juice

Extra virgin olive oil

Salt and pepper

Place the bulgur wheat in the pot with the chicken stock, making sure it is at least half an inch above the height of the wheat. Boil for 10 minutes, until soft.

Fluff up the bulgur with a fork and add the onion and the herbs, stirring through.

Sprinkle with some lemon juice, drizzle with a little extra virgin olive oil and season. Mix well before serving.

QUINOA SUPERFOOD SALAD

This salad will leave you feeling virtuous but also very satisfied. It's crunchy, zesty, salty and delicious! If you are ever feeling run down and tired, this is a great one to perk you up. I'm including my method to cook lovely nutty quinoa without the soggy texture many people tell me they end up with!

SERVES 8–10 AS A SIDE

30g quinoa

Chicken or vegetable stock (enough to more than cover the quinoa)

200g green beans

120g peas, fresh or frozen

Salt

100g cucumber, diced

100g good-quality feta cheese, crumbled

20g alfalfa sprouts (optional)

20g toasted seeds (sesame, flax, sunflower and/or pumpkin)

50g avocado, cut into pieces

A small handful of flat-leaf parsley, roughly chopped

A small handful of mint, roughly chopped

2 tablespoons lemon juice

4 tablespoons extra virgin olive oil

Place the quinoa in a pot and cover to an inch above the surface of the grain with the chicken or vegetable stock. Boil for 10 minutes or until small holes appear on the surface. Turn the heat off and cover – DO NOT STIR.

Leave to steam for another 10 minutes. Fluff up with a fork and allow to cool to room temperature before using.

Put enough boiling water to cover the green beans and peas into a saucepan with a pinch of salt. Bring back to the boil, then drop in the green beans and peas and put the lid back on. Cook for 3 minutes, then drain and run under cold water to take all the heat out. This keeps them vibrant and green.

Now build your salad in layers, starting with the quinoa, then the vegetables, the feta, the sprouts (if using) and seeds, the avocado and finally the herbs.

Put the lemon juice and oil in a jar and shake well to combine. Dress the salad just before it is to be eaten.

DESSERT

CARAMELISED PINEAPPLE WITH CHOCOLATE SAUCE

MAKES 12 PIECES

There is only really one dessert that is worth making on the barbecue and that is caramelised fruit. Pineapple is one of the best, and, inspired by Nigella, I have found that you can't beat this when it is served with a gorgeous chocolate sauce.

● • ● • ● • ● • ● • ● • ● • ● • ●

1 ripe pineapple

250g demerara sugar

200g dark chocolate (minimum 70% cocoa solids)

120ml double cream

You will need enough skewers to hold twelve pieces of pineapple, soaked in cold water to stop them catching fire in the heat of the barbecue.

Cut the top and bottom off the pineapple and, working vertically, slice the skin off the fruit.

Cut into quarters and then into about three pieces again, lengthways, so that you have twelve wedges of pineapple.

Cut out the woody core, thread the wedges onto each soaked skewer lengthways and arrange flat in a shallow dish until ready to cook.

Lay the pineapple kebabs on a sheet of foil and thickly coat them with demerara sugar. Then place them on the barbecue until the sugar caramelises and the fruit scorches.

Meanwhile, put the chocolate, broken up into pieces, into a thick-bottomed pan and melt over a low heat. Then, stirring continuously, pour in the cream, plus any juice that has gathered from the fruit. When the sauce is thick, smooth and hot, pour into a bowl with a ladle, or enough little bowls to give one to each person.

Take the kebabs off the barbecue, lay them on a large plate and let everyone take them as they want, dipping the pineapple into the hot chocolate sauce as they eat.

STRESS-FREE SUNDAY ROASTS

THERE IS NOTHING LIKE A SUNDAY ROAST WITH THE FAMILY TO FINISH OFF THE WEEK. MY FATHER MAKES THE BEST SUNDAY ROAST WITH ALL THE TRIMMINGS, WHICH HASN'T CHANGED SINCE CHILDHOOD AND TAKES A LOT OF EFFORT. THE RECIPES IN THIS CHAPTER WILL HOPEFULLY GIVE YOU A GREAT SUNDAY ROAST WITHOUT ALL THE EFFORT! THE BONUS OF THESE RECIPES IS THAT THE LEFTOVERS CAN BE USED DURING THE WEEK. I ALWAYS MAKE EXTRA POTATOES, MEAT AND GRAVY WHILE I HAVE THE TIME, SPECIFICALLY FOR THIS PURPOSE.

TIMING YOUR ROAST

· · · · · · · · · ·

One thing many people at my classes tell me they find stressful about Sunday roasts is timing everything to get it to the table at its best. I usually start my vegetables while the meat is resting and the roast potatoes are still in the oven. That way you are only working on the vegetables at the last minute.

SUGGESTED TIMETABLE OF WORK FOR A STRESS-FREE SUNDAY ROAST (FOR LEG OF LAMB, LOIN OF PORK AND RIB OF BEEF)

2 hours before serving	→	Start the gravy by caramelising the onions while waiting for the oven to preheat.
1 hour 45 minutes before serving	→	Get the joint into oven. However, do allow a little extra time here if you have a bigger joint.
1 hour 30 minutes before serving	→	Start the roast potatoes.
30 minutes before serving	→	Remove the meat from the oven. Start the vegetables. Finish the gravy with the meat juices.

ITALIAN-STYLE ROAST LOIN OF PORK WITH MARSALA GRAVY + STIR-FRIED KALE

A really quick and easy dish that has a great flavour and can be made with minimum fuss.

SERVES 6-8

1.5kg pork loin, boned and rolled

4 cloves of garlic, crushed

2 tablespoons fennel seeds

1 tablespoon chopped rosemary leaves

1 tablespoon chopped thyme leaves

A pinch of salt and pepper

1 tablespoon vegetable oil

Rapeseed oil

A knob of butter

1 head of kale, washed and roughly torn

½ lemon

FOR THE MARSALA GRAVY:

A knob of butter

Salt

2 handfuls of sliced mushrooms

1 heaped tablespoon plain flour

1 teaspoon tomato purée

50ml Marsala

150ml chicken stock

1 teaspoon redcurrant jelly

Preheat the oven to 200°C/fan 180°C/gas mark 6.

Place the pork in a roasting tray and put into the oven for 20 minutes. Reduce the heat to 180°C/fan 160°C/gas mark 4 for 45 minutes per kilo.

Place the garlic, fennel seeds, rosemary, thyme and seasoning into a mortar and pestle. Grind until blended well, add the vegetable oil, then rub into the pork meat for the last 30 minutes of cooking. A silicone brush is handy for this.

Once cooked, remove the meat from the roasting tray and allow to rest while making the gravy.

Melt the butter in the roasting tray on the hob with a pinch of salt. Add the sliced mushrooms and cook for 5 minutes.

Add the flour, stir through and cook for another minute, then add the tomato purée and the Marsala and allow to absorb into the mushrooms for a minute.

Pour in the stock. Bring to the boil, stirring, then add the redcurrant jelly. Stir until dissolved. Season with salt and pepper to taste. If you want a rustic gravy then you can serve it with the mushrooms in it, or for a smooth liquid you can strain the gravy into a warm sauceboat.

To prepare the kale, heat a large frying pan or wok over a medium heat. Add a glug of rapeseed oil and a knob of butter. When the butter is foaming, add the kale, stirring regularly until wilted. Squeeze a generous amount of lemon juice over and serve straight away with the pork and gravy. This is delicious with roast potatoes (see p. 201) or rustic herby roast potatoes (see p. 166).

MUM'S BEER POT ROAST

SERVES 4–6

This is my mum's recipe and is a real comfort food for all our family. She has been making it for years and she insists on using Smithwicks, but feel free to change the type of ale.

• • • • • • • • • • • • •

1.3kg topside, brisket or top rib of beef

1 tablespoon plain flour, seasoned with salt and pepper

A knob of butter

3 streaky rashers of bacon, diced

1 onion, finely diced

3 sticks of celery, chopped into large chunks

3 carrots, chopped into large chunks

1 can of ale

Preheat the oven to 140°C/fan 120°C/gas mark 1.

Using kitchen roll, dry the beef. Sprinkle the seasoned flour on a plate and roll the beef in the flour until coated.

Melt a good knob of butter over a medium heat in a heavy-based, ovenproof pot and sauté the bacon until the fat is rendered (i.e. the bacon is crisping up). Using a slotted spoon, remove the bacon and set aside.

Using tongs, brown the beef on all sides in the butter and bacon fat. Remove from the heat and set aside.

Add all the vegetables to the pot and sauté, adding a little more butter if the pot has dried out. Cook for approximately 5 minutes or until softened, stirring occasionally. Add the beer and bubble to deglaze the pot, then put the beef and bacon back into the pot.

Spoon the cooking broth over the beef and place in the oven for 2½ hours. After an hour, turn the beef in the broth and spoon over the juices.

When cooked, remove from the oven and leave to rest for 15 minutes or so. Remove the beef from the juices and carve. Serve with the vegetables and juices, accompanied by fluffy mashed potatoes and extra vegetables, like orange-glazed carrots (see p. 203), or green beans with lemon and garlic (see p. 204).

LEMON ROAST CHICKEN

SERVES 4

The great thing about this roast chicken is the lack of chopping or prep you need to do while it still delivers on great flavour. Use the leftovers for Thai chicken noodle broth (see p. 209), Vietnamese spring rolls (see p. 106), quiche cups (see p. 224) or quesadillas (see p. 85).

• • • • • • • • • • • • •

1.5kg chicken

1 lemon, cut in half

3 or 4 sprigs of herbs, such as thyme, rosemary, bay leaf, parsley (your choice)

Olive oil

Salt and pepper

15g butter

15g plain flour

Preheat the oven to 200°C/fan 180°C/gas mark 6.

Place the chicken in a roasting dish, place half the lemon and some herbs inside the cavity and rub a little olive oil all over the skin. Season with salt and pepper.

Cook in the oven for 1½ to 2 hours until cooked through – the best way to check this is to put a large fork into the cavity and hold the chicken up carefully. If the juices run clear then it is cooked. Place the chicken in a warm place to rest before serving, reserving the juices in the roasting dish.

Squeeze the juice of the other half of the lemon into the roasting juices.

Make the roux by melting the butter in a pot over a medium heat. Add the flour, combine and cook for 5 minutes. Add a tablespoon of the roux to the juices in the roasting dish over a high heat whisking vigorously. Allow to come to the boil. The juices should have thickened to give a good consistency, but add a little more of the roux if it is still too liquid for your liking. If it has become too thick, add a couple of tablespoons of hot water.

Serve with roast potatoes (see p. 201) and roast Tabasco cauliflower à la Kristiina (see p. 202).

HONEY + MUSTARD ROAST GAMMON WITH CHAMP

The ultimate traditional Irish dish.

SERVES 4

2 tablespoons honey

1 teaspoon English mustard

1 gammon (approx. 750g)

500g potatoes

A generous knob of butter

Salt and white pepper (optional)

4 tablespoons milk

3 spring onions, finely chopped

Preheat the oven to 160°C/fan 140°C/gas mark 3.

Mix the honey and mustard together to make a glaze.

Place the gammon in an ovenproof dish and pour the glaze over. Bake for about 45 minutes or until cooked through (this depends on the thickness of the gammon). If the meat is cooked, when you insert a skewer into the centre and immediately check the tip with your fingers, it will be hot.

In the meantime, peel the potatoes and boil until softened. Drain well and mash with the butter, adding a little salt and white pepper if you like. Set aside.

Boil the milk and add to the potato, together with the spring onions, and mix through.

Allow the gammon to rest for 10 minutes before slicing. Carve the meat and serve with the mash. To keep it traditional, serve with boiled cabbage.

ROAST LEG OF LAMB

Nothing says Mother's Day, Easter and brighter days like a roast leg of lamb.

• • • • • • • • • • • •

1 leg of lamb (1.5kg)

1 tablespoon rapeseed oil (approx.)

3 cloves of garlic, sliced

A couple of rosemary sprigs

Salt and pepper

1 carrot, cut into chunks

1 onion, quartered

1 stick of celery, cut into chunks

A few drops of soy sauce

A few drops of Worcestershire sauce

FOR THE GRAVY:

15g butter

1 small onion, finely diced

A pinch of salt

1 teaspoon tomato purée

15g plain flour

A dash of red wine

250ml lamb stock

Preheat the oven to 180°C/fan 160°C/gas mark 4.

Placing the lamb on a board, use the sharp tip of a small knife to make incisions about ½cm deep all around the leg. Brush with a little rapeseed oil, then poke the garlic and bits of the rosemary into the holes. Season the lamb generously.

Place the carrot, onion and celery into a roasting dish and add a little soy sauce, Worcestershire sauce and a cup of water. Place the lamb on top and roast in the oven for 2 hours.

To make the gravy, melt the butter in a saucepan, then add the onion with a pinch of salt and cook on a medium heat with the lid on until the onion softens and starts to caramelise – this will take up to 10 minutes.

Add the tomato purée, stir and cook for 2 minutes, then add the flour. Cook for 1–2 minutes, then add the wine and allow to bubble until almost evaporated. Add the lamb stock and reduce to a simmer for at least 30 minutes, stirring every now and then.

When the meat is done, remove the lamb to a warmed dish to rest (for at least 10 minutes) and pour the juices from the roasting dish into the gravy. The gravy should now be rich and flavourful. If you wish, pour through a sieve for a smoother finish. Serve with roast potatoes and vegetables of your choice.

ROAST RIB OF BEEF

SERVES 6

2kg rib of beef on the bone

1 tablespoon plain flour

1 teaspoon mustard powder

1 teaspoon ground black pepper

1 onion, quartered with the skin left on

1 carrot, washed and chopped into 4 pieces

2 sticks of celery

Soy sauce

Worcestershire sauce

FOR THE GRAVY:

A knob of butter

1 small onion, finely diced

1 teaspoon tomato purée

1 tablespoon flour

250ml beef stock

Here is a helpful guide for finishing the cooking:

Rare	10–12 mins per 450g or 1lb
Medium	12–15 mins per 450g or 1lb
Well done	18–20 mins per 450g or 1lb

• • • • • • • • • • • • •

Bring the beef to room temperature before cooking for the best results. Preheat the oven to 240°C/fan 220°C/gas mark 9.

Mix together the flour, mustard powder and pepper and rub the mixture all over the beef.

Place the onion, carrot and celery in the bottom of a large roasting dish. Sprinkle a little soy sauce and Worcestershire sauce over the vegetable mixture and top with the rib of beef. Finally, add boiling water to the roasting dish until it is about 1½cm in depth.

Cook the beef for 25 minutes on this temperature. Then reduce the temperature to 180°C/fan 160°C/gas mark 4 until the meat is cooked to your taste – see the table above. If you insert a skewer into the middle of the meat and check the colour of the juices, red, pink or clear will indicate rare, medium or well done.

To make the gravy, melt the butter in a saucepan and add the onion. Sauté gently until soft and add the tomato purée and cook for a minute or so. Add the flour and continue cooking for about 3 minutes, stirring, then add the beef stock and keep on a low simmer until the meat is cooked.

When the beef is cooked to your liking, remove from the roasting dish and allow to rest for 15–30 minutes in a warm place before you carve it.

While the beef rests, strain the onions out of the gravy and put the strained liquid back in the pot. Add the meat juices and reduce by simmering.

Carve the meat in thin slices and serve with the gravy, roast potatoes (see p. 201) and any of the vegetable sides from this chapter.

SIDES

CLASSIC ROAST POTATOES

This is my method for crispy on the outside, fluffy in the centre potatoes. Make sure you time these to be served straight from the oven, in other words, give your meat time to rest. All you need is potatoes and rapeseed oil. I am not giving quantities for the potatoes as it depends on how many people you are cooking for and how many potatoes you like. If you are doing a lot, you may need to increase the amount of oil. I am a glutton for roast potatoes. Leftovers of these are also great for making potato hash.

• • • • • • • • • • • • • • •

Rooster potatoes
2–3 tablespoons rapeseed oil

Preheat the oven to 200°C/fan 180°C/gas mark 6.

Peel the potatoes and cut into even-sized chunks. Place in a saucepan and cover with cold water. Bring to the boil and allow to cook for about 3 minutes.

In the meantime, pour the rapeseed oil into an ovenproof dish big enough for the amount of potatoes you are doing and place in the oven.

Empty the boiled potatoes into a colander and place a clean tea towel over them. Holding the tea towel over the colander in the sink, give them a good shake to bash up the edges. This will help to make them lovely and crispy.

Carefully put the potatoes into the preheated oil. The oil should be good and hot and you should hear a little sizzle when you put the potatoes in. Brush the potatoes with some of the oil, making sure all of the potatoes are well coated.

Roast for about 1 hour and 15 minutes, shaking every now and then to ensure they brown evenly.

ROAST TABASCO CAULIFLOWER À LA KRISTIINA

SERVES 4

1 head of cauliflower cut into bite-sized florets

Tabasco sauce

Olive oil

Salt

This recipe was a revelation for me when the lovely Kristiina, a friend of the family, made it for our Sunday roast. It is so easy and has become a staple in our house.

• • • • • • • • • • • •

Preheat the oven to 180˚C /fan 160˚C/gas mark 4.

Put the cauliflower in a roasting dish and sprinkle over as much Tabasco as you want, depending on how spicy you like it.

Drizzle with a little olive oil, season with salt and roast for 15–20 minutes, until al dente or soft, depending on how you like it.

ORANGE–GLAZED CARROTS WITH TARRAGON

SERVES 4

500g carrots, cut into 1-inch chunks on the diagonal

Juice of 1 large orange

A knob of butter

1 tablespoon brown sugar

4 sprigs of fresh tarragon

My friend Paula made these for me years ago and the combination of fresh orange juice and tarragon was a revelation. If you can't find tarragon, use parsley instead.

• ● • ● • ● • ● • ● • ● • ●

Preheat the oven to 200°C/fan 180°C/gas mark 6.

Place all the ingredients, except the tarragon, into a roasting dish and cook until soft and glazed (about 40 minutes depending on the thickness of the carrots).

Chop the tarragon leaves and scatter over just before serving.

GREEN BEANS WITH LEMON + GARLIC

SERVES 4

This is a lovely light way to serve green beans. They are a great accompaniment to rich meats and gravy as they are slightly bitter, giving a lovely balance.

• ● • ● • ● • ● • ● • ● • ●

A knob of butter

1 clove of garlic, roughly chopped

500g green beans, blanched

½ lemon

Salt and pepper

Place the butter in a pan over a medium heat until foaming, then add the garlic and green beans, and toss. Add a squeeze of lemon juice, season to taste and serve.

MEAL-IN-A-BOWL SUPER SOUPS

• • • • • • • • • • • • • • • • • •

MAKING A BIG POT OF SOUP IS IN ITSELF A STRESS RELIEVER FOR ME. IT SLOWS YOU DOWN AND THE ANTICIPATION OF A BOWL OF COMFORTING SOUP IMMEDIATELY SOOTHES THE SOUL. I'M NOT THE ONLY ONE WHO THINKS LIKE THIS — JUST LOOK AT JACK CANFIELD AND MARK HANSEN'S SERIES OF *CHICKEN SOUP FOR THE SOUL* BOOKS. TO REALLY TAKE THE STRESS OUT OF MAKING SOUP, USE YOUR FOOD PROCESSOR TO BLITZ THE VEGETABLES, AS THIS WILL SAVE YOU CHOPPING AND ALSO MEANS THEY WILL SWEAT DOWN FASTER. ALL THESE SOUPS CAN BE FROZEN, SO IF YOU MAKE A BIG BATCH YOU CAN JUST DEFROST THESE WHEN YOU HAVE NO TIME TO MAKE THEM.

THAI CHICKEN NOODLE BROTH

I crave this when I am sick with a cold or flu, or simply a bit tired and stressed. I am not mad about the term 'clean eating' but it does describe this pretty well. This is a great way to use up leftover roast chicken if you have it, but if you don't you can use chicken fillets as per the recipe below. If you have roast chicken left over, simply shred it and add it in for the last minute of cooking to heat it through.

SERVES 2

• • • • • • • • • • • • • • •

750ml chicken or vegetable stock

1 chicken fillet, sliced into bite-sized pieces

1 tablespoon nam pla (Thai fish sauce)

Juice of 1 lime or lemon

1 clove of garlic, finely sliced

1 large piece of ginger, peeled and sliced

1 nest of medium egg noodles

3 handfuls of mixed vegetables (e.g. baby sweetcorn, mangetout, pak choi, spinach, peppers, sugar snaps, beansprouts)

1 fresh red chilli, sliced (optional)

A small bunch of coriander or flat-leaf parsley, chopped

2 spring onions, sliced

Put the stock into a large pot and bring to the boil. Place the chicken, nam pla, lime/lemon juice, garlic and ginger into it and poach over a medium heat for 3–4 minutes or until the chicken has turned white. Make sure the water is not boiling too hard or the chicken will break up.

Add the noodles and the harder vegetables, such as the corn (if using) and peppers. Poach for another 3–4 minutes.

Remove a large piece of chicken and slice in half to check that it is cooked through. If it is cooked, switch off the heat.

Add the leafy greens and any other vegetables you are using and stir through. Taste for balance between the citrus juice and nam pla. Adjust to your liking by adding more nam pla or citrus if necessary.

Ladle into bowls, ensuring a good mix of all the ingredients with the poaching liquid. When serving, sprinkle with the chilli (if using), herbs and spring onions.

MOROCCAN HARIRA WITH GARLIC + CHILLI PRAWNS

I love having leftover soup, whatever the time of year, as it is both filling and light. I have been doing this soup in my 'Foods of North Africa and the North East' class for years now and it is a great one to make a double portion and freeze half.

SERVES 6

• • • • • • • • • • • • •

Olive oil

1 onion, finely chopped

2 cloves of garlic, finely chopped

250g red split lentils

1 x 400g tin of chickpeas

2½ litres of chicken or vegetable stock

1 x 400g tin of chopped tomatoes

¼ teaspoon ground cinnamon

¼ teaspoon ground ginger

1 good pinch of saffron, lightly toasted and crushed

60ml sherry

Juice and zest of 1 lemon

A handful of fresh parsley, coriander and celery leaves, chopped

Salt and pepper

TO GARNISH (OPTIONAL):

12 prawns

¼ teaspoon dried chilli flakes

2 cloves of garlic, minced

1 tablespoon olive oil

Heat a glug of olive oil in a large saucepan and sweat the onion for about 5 minutes. Add the garlic and cook until softened.

Add the lentils and chickpeas and 2 litres of the stock and boil for 15 minutes. Blend using a stick blender, but leave it a little rough. Add the tinned tomatoes, cinnamon, ginger and saffron and bring to the boil.

Add the sherry, lemon juice and zest. Adjust the consistency of the soup with the remaining stock if necessary, then add the fresh herbs, season and serve.

To make the garnish for the soup, combine the prawns with the chilli, garlic and olive oil. Heat a frying pan until hot and toss the prawns until cooked through and opaque. Be careful not to overcook them or they will become tough!

Serve the soup in bowls with some of the garnish spooned on top.

MULLIGATAWNY

SERVES 6

This really is a gorgeously comforting 'meal in a bowl'. I love this on a cold winter's afternoon. Another great one for the freezer! This is lovely served with the naan bread on page 165.

• • • • • • • • • • • •

1 onion, sliced

1 teaspoon groundnut oil

Salt

2 cloves of garlic, chopped

1 thumb-sized piece of fresh ginger, grated

1 teaspoon turmeric

1 teaspoon ground cumin

1 teaspoon garam masala

½ teaspoon allspice

A pinch of dried chilli flakes

1 teaspoon tomato purée

200g red split lentils

1 x 400g tin of chickpeas

750ml chicken stock

Juice of ½ lime

Natural yoghurt

A small bunch of fresh coriander, chopped

Sweat the onion in the oil with a pinch of salt. When softened (this will take at least 5 minutes), add the garlic, ginger and spices.

Cook for 2–3 minutes, stirring, then add the tomato purée, lentils and chickpeas, coating them in the lovely flavour base. Add the stock and bring to the boil.

Reduce the heat and simmer for about 10–15 minutes or until the lentils are soft. Blitz with a stick blender. Add a little more stock or water if it is too thick. Add a squeeze of lime juice and taste for seasoning, adding a little salt if required.

Garnish with a dollop of yoghurt and some fresh coriander.

MINESTRONE SOUP

SERVES 8

A great meal in a bowl for all ages. Soup mix can be found in most supermarkets.

• • • • • • • • • • • • •

Rapeseed oil

1 large onion, finely chopped

A good pinch of sea salt

2 cloves of garlic, finely chopped

A good pinch of dried chilli flakes

A sprig of fresh thyme and oregano, chopped, or 1 teaspoon each of the dried herbs

3 tablespoons 'soup mix'

2 stalks of celery, chopped

2 large carrots, chopped into small chunks

1 red pepper, seeded and diced

1 yellow pepper, seeded and diced

1 x 400g tin of chopped tomatoes

2 litres chicken stock

75g spaghetti, broken into 1-inch pieces

1 x 400g tin of cannellini beans

In a large pot, heat a good glug of the rapeseed oil and sauté the onion with the salt until it becomes soft. Add the garlic, chilli flakes, herbs and 'soup mix' and sauté for another minute or so.

Stir in the celery, carrots and peppers and cook for 5 minutes. Add the chopped tomatoes and chicken stock and bring to the boil, then reduce the heat and simmer for 20 minutes.

Add the spaghetti and cannellini beans. Give the soup a good stir and cover.

Cook gently for a further 10 minutes or until the pasta is cooked.

THAI BUTTERNUT SQUASH SOUP

SERVES 4-6

One of my favourite soups, a lovely warming dish especially in the winter.

• • • • • • • • • • • • •

1 portion Thai curry paste
(see p. 50 or shop-bought)

Rapeseed oil

1 onion, chopped

Salt

1 clove of garlic

1 butternut squash, cut into small
cubes

1 small sweet potato, cut into
small cubes

400ml vegetable/chicken stock

200ml coconut milk (the rest of
the tin can be frozen)

A bunch of fresh coriander,
chopped

Pepper (optional)

First make the curry paste (see p. 50).

To make the soup, heat a large saucepan. When good and hot, add some oil and sweat the onion with a pinch of salt for 5 minutes.

Add the garlic and continue to cook for 1 minute, then add the butternut squash and sweet potato and sauté for 5 minutes.

Stir through 2 tablespoons of the curry paste to coat the vegetables thoroughly.

Pour in the stock, cover and simmer for at least 10 minutes. Check the vegetables are soft by inserting a knife into them.

Blend either with a stick blender or in a food processor, return to the pot and add the coconut milk and fresh coriander. Season if required and serve.

FRAGRANT PEA + LEMONGRASS SOUP

SERVES 4-6

A fantastic, light and speedy soup that takes just 10 minutes to make. This is a lovely meal for the summer months. Note: this is also fabulous as a beetroot soup. Just add four cooked vacuum-packed beetroots instead of the peas and simmer for 15 minutes, then proceed as below. It is a good idea, before you start, to check how hot your chillis are, as they can vary in strength.

• • • • • • • • • • • •

1 onion

1 clove of garlic

2 stalks of lemongrass

1 red chilli, deseeded

1 thumb-sized piece of ginger

Rapeseed oil

850ml chicken or vegetable stock

450g peas, fresh or frozen

Nam pla (Thai fish sauce)

½ lime

Some fresh coriander

A little crème fraîche (optional)

Place the onion, garlic, lemongrass, chilli and ginger in a food processor and blitz until well chopped.

Heat some oil in a large saucepan, add the blitzed vegetables and sweat over a medium heat for 2–3 minutes until soft. Pour in the stock and bring the soup to the boil.

Add the peas and bring the liquid back to the boil. The peas do not need to be cooked any more than this or they can lose their vibrancy.

Blitz with a stick blender until fairly smooth. Season with some nam pla and lime juice to taste. When serving, top with the coriander and a little crème fraîche if desired.

CURRIED PARSNIP + APPLE SOUP

SERVES 4-6

We started making this soup in our Christmas classes and found both adults and children alike loved it. I was surprised that kids liked it so much but I think a little sharp sweetness from the apple did the trick.

• • • • • • • • • • • • •

30g butter

1 tablespoon rapeseed oil

1 onion, chopped

Salt

2 large cooking apples, peeled, cored and chopped

4–5 parsnips, chopped

1 clove of garlic, chopped

1 teaspoon ground coriander

1 teaspoon ground cumin

1 teaspoon ground ginger

1½ litres vegetable stock

Pepper

A dash of cream

Melt the butter with the oil in a large pan, then add the onion with a pinch of salt. Cook for at least 5 minutes until softened. Add the apples and parsnips and cook for a further 3–4 minutes. Add the garlic, coriander, cumin and ginger and stir for 30 seconds.

Pour in the stock, season well and bring to the boil. Reduce the heat, cover and simmer for 15–20 minutes, or until the parsnip is soft.

Remove from the heat, then blend until smooth.

Stir in the cream and reheat gently, but don't boil, before serving.

MULTI-SEED TRADITIONAL IRISH WHEATEN BREAD

It is always nice to have a go-to brown-bread recipe. This really is very easy to make and sometimes I make a double batch, one for the freezer and one for now. For me, there is nothing nicer to accompany a steaming bowl of soup. If you don't have buttermilk, sour the same quantity of milk by adding a teaspoon of white wine vinegar, lemon juice or cream of tartar and leaving to sit out in the kitchen for 45 minutes. It is important to do this as the bread soda reacts to the acidity and makes the bread nice and light.

MAKES 1 LOAF

50g butter, plus extra for greasing

350g wholemeal flour

100g plain flour

40g porridge oats

1½ teaspoons bread soda

1 teaspoon salt

50g mixed seeds of your choice (e.g. sesame, poppy, linseed, sunflower or pumpkin)

2 tablespoons wheat bran

500ml buttermilk

1 tablespoon honey

Preheat the oven to 220°C/fan 200°C/gas mark 7.

Grease a 900g/2lb loaf tin with a little melted butter and line the bottom with parchment paper.

Place the flours, oats, bread soda, salt, seeds and wheat bran into a large mixing bowl.

Melt the butter in a pot or jug and add the buttermilk and honey.

Stir the wet ingredients into the dry ingredients in the large bowl. Mix gently to make a soft dough.

Shape lightly and place in the loaf tin. If you like, sprinkle with a few extra seeds for decoration.

Bake for 10 minutes, then reduce the oven temperature to 200°C/fan 180°C/gas mark 6 and bake for a further 20–30 minutes, until golden and firm to the touch.

Carefully (using oven gloves or a tea towel) turn out the bread from the tin – when it's done, it should sound hollow when the base is tapped. Leave to cool on a wire rack before slicing.

COOKING WITH KIDS

· · · · · · · · · · · · · · ·

I JUST HAD TO INCLUDE A CHAPTER ON COOKING WITH KIDS BECAUSE I RUN SO MANY KIDS' COOKERY CLASSES AND I HAVE FOUND CHILDREN JUST LOVE COOKING. THEY ALSO TEND TO BE MUCH BETTER EATERS IN TERMS OF VARIETY OF FOODS WHEN THEY ARE INVOLVED IN THE COOKING. IT'S LOVELY TO ALLOW THE KIDS TO EXPLORE THEIR CREATIVE SIDE BY TASTING AND TESTING AS THEY GO ALONG. I ALSO THINK IT'S A GREAT WAY TO GET CHILDREN SET UP FOR HEALTHIER EATING HABITS IN LATER LIFE WHEN THEY CAN COOK FROM SCRATCH.

HOMEMADE BAKED BEANS

SERVES 2-4

Hardly a recipe but delicious nonetheless! I really wanted to include this as kids tend to love baked beans but they are often full of sugar, so these are a much healthier and wholesome option. As a light lunch this serves four younger or two older children.

• • • • • • • • • • • •

1 x 400g tin of cannellini beans

2 tablespoons Parmesan, grated (optional)

FOR THE TOMATO SAUCE:

2 tablespoons olive oil

1 onion, finely chopped

1 clove of garlic, crushed

1 x 400g tin of chopped tomatoes

1 teaspoon sugar

Salt and pepper

First make the tomato sauce. Heat the oil in a saucepan, gently cook the onion and then add the garlic until soft (not coloured) – this should take about 5 minutes. Stir in the tomatoes and sugar. Bring to a simmer and cook gently for 15–20 minutes.

Season with salt and pepper, then whiz in a food processor or with a stick blender until smooth.

Pop a tin of cannellini beans into a small ovenproof dish and top with the sauce. Bake at 180°C/fan 160°C/gas mark 4 for 10–15 minutes. You can pop some grated Parmesan on top before baking to make it a bit more robust! This is really a side dish, but can make a light lunch or tea when served with some crusty bread and a green salad.

SPICY TOMATO + BASIL SOUP

SERVES 6

Omit the chilli if your kids don't like it, but it's really just a very gentle heat.

• ● • ● • ● • ● • ● • ●

Rapeseed oil

1 onion, diced

Salt

1 clove of garlic, chopped

1 teaspoon tomato purée

½ teaspoon dried chilli flakes

1 x 400g tin of tomatoes

1 teaspoon sugar

250ml chicken stock

Pepper

A dash of cream (optional)

6 fresh basil leaves (approx.), torn

Heat a glug of oil in a large pan, then sweat off the onion with a little salt until softened. Add the garlic, the tomato purée and chilli flakes and cook for a few moments.

Pour in the tin of tomatoes and add the sugar. Bring to the boil and add the stock. Boil for 5–10 minutes or until the flavour has developed. Blend until smooth. Season to taste.

Add a dash of cream (if using) to the pot just before serving and whisk through. Garnish with the basil when serving.

QUICHE CUPS

This dish is full of protein and delicious. The use of a tortilla wrap as a base for these eggy bites makes for a great lunchbox addition for school (or work for the adults!) and helps keep the energy levels up.

• • • • • • • • • • • • •

MAKES 6

1 wholemeal wrap

3 eggs

50ml cream

Salt and pepper

Any fillings you fancy (e.g. grated Parmesan, ham, bacon, sautéed mushrooms, herbs, bacon, tomatoes or my favourite combo: feta, mint and sautéed courgettes)

Preheat the oven to 180˚C/fan 160˚C/gas mark 4.

You will need a six-hole muffin tin. Cut the wholemeal wrap into six circles large enough to fill the holes in the muffin tin, and place in the tin.

Whisk the eggs with the cream in a jug or bowl with a pouring spout. Season and add whatever fillings you are using.

Pour the mixture about two-thirds of the way up to the top of the muffin holes, then bake for about 10 minutes or until the filling is puffed up and cooked through.

THAI FISH CAKES

You can either shallow fry, deep-fry or oven bake these cakes: I like to start them in a frying pan to crisp them up and then finish them in the oven.

• • • • • • • • • • • • • •

200g fish fillets, no skin (e.g. cod, haddock, salmon or smoked haddock)

2 teaspoons nam pla (Thai fish sauce)

1 teaspoon cumin

A small bunch of fresh coriander, chopped

1 tablespoon fresh lime juice

1 clove of garlic

Salt and pepper

1 small egg, beaten

3 tablespoons milk

3 tablespoons plain flour

A couple of large handfuls of breadcrumbs

Rapeseed oil (or any other high-burning-point oil)

Chilli crème fraîche (see p. 127)

Slice the fish into chunks. Put it into a food processor with the nam pla, cumin, coriander, lime juice, garlic, salt and pepper to taste, and half of the beaten egg. Blitz for about 10 seconds.

Check the mixture has bound together and add a little more of the egg and blitz again if necessary.

Divide the mixture into four patties and chill them for an hour if you have time – this will help them firm up.

Preheat the oven to 180°C/fan 160°C/gas mark 4.

Place the remaining egg and the milk in a large shallow bowl and mix. Place the flour in another bowl and the breadcrumbs in another.

Put the fish cakes in the flour, shaking off the excess, then dip them in the eggy milk mixture and finally in the breadcrumbs.

Heat a frying pan and add a couple of tablespoons of oil. Fry the fish cakes over a medium heat in batches for 1 minute on each side. When they are golden, drain on kitchen paper and place on a baking tray. Bake in the oven for 10–15 minutes depending on the thickness of the cakes.

While the fish cakes are baking, make the chilli crème fraîche (see p. 127).

Serve with a few green salad leaves and some chilli crème fraîche.

CHEESE + HERB-CRUSTED BAKED SALMON

SERVES 4

This is another winner at our kids' cookery camps and has convinced many 'no fish' eaters to change their minds.

• • • • • • • • • • • • •

50g breadcrumbs

3 tablespoons grated Parmesan or strong cheddar

1 teaspoon dried mixed herbs

50g butter, melted

Salt and pepper

4 salmon fillets

2 tablespoons mayonnaise

Place the breadcrumbs, Parmesan, herbs and butter into a bowl and combine. Season to taste.

Place the fish onto an ovenproof dish, smear with the mayonnaise and top with the breadcrumb mixture.

Place in the oven for 15–20 minutes depending on the thickness of your fish. Once the fish is cooked, serve with the oven-roasted wedges on page 72 and a green salad.

STICKY CHICKEN DRUMSTICKS

SERVES 4

These drumsticks are always an absolute winner at our kids' cookery camps. They are also ideal finger food for birthday parties.

• • • • • • • • • • • •

2 tablespoons soy sauce

2 tablespoons honey

½ teaspoon paprika

½ teaspoon ground coriander

1 clove of garlic, minced

1 thumb-sized piece of ginger, grated

8 chicken drumsticks

Combine the soy sauce, honey, paprika, coriander, garlic and ginger in a bowl.

Score the skin of the chicken drumsticks a couple of times and place in an ovenproof dish. Pour the marinade over them, ensuring all the chicken pieces are coated. Marinate for as long as possible, but at least 30 minutes.

Preheat the oven to 180°C/fan 160°C/gas mark 4.

Cook in the oven for 30 minutes. I love to serve this with sticky basmati rice (see p. 167) and some salad.

CHICKEN FAJITAS

SERVES 4

This is an all-time favourite amongst the kids at our cookery camp and I get children who have done them with me before asking to do them again. You can buy fajita packs if you don't have time to make the spice mix, salsa and tortilla wraps, but it's much nicer if you make them yourself and kids usually love making the dough!

• • • • • • • • • • • •

1 portion of tomato salsa
(see p. 95)

2 chicken fillets

½ red pepper, sliced lengthways

½ onion, sliced

Groundnut or rapeseed oil

Some cheddar cheese, grated

Sour cream

FOR THE HOMEMADE TORTILLA WRAPS:

250g plain flour

½ teaspoon salt

3 tablespoons olive oil

175ml water

FOR THE SPICE MIX:

1 teaspoon sea salt

1 teaspoon caster sugar

1 teaspoon ground cumin

1 teaspoon ground coriander

½ teaspoon chilli powder

½ teaspoon dried oregano

½ teaspoon ground black pepper

½ teaspoon paprika

To make the tortilla wraps, put the flour and salt in a bowl and mix. Make a little well in the middle, add the oil and water, mix it all together and knead the resulting dough for about 10 minutes. Shape the dough into a ball and put it back in the bowl, cover with cling film and leave in a warm place for at least half an hour (or even overnight if you want).

Prepare the spice mix by combining all the ingredients, then set aside.

Make the tomato salsa by combining all the ingredients (see p. 95), then set aside.

When you are ready to cook the tortillas, put the dough out on a floured worktop. Cut the dough into four golfball-sized pieces and roll these out into circles, as thin as possible.

Heat a dry frying pan and place your tortilla wrap into it. When it starts to blister and bubble, carefully turn it over and cook the other side. Do be careful, as steam can pop out suddenly.

When all the tortillas are cooked, prepare the filling. Slice the chicken fillets into about six pieces each. Place the chicken, pepper and onion in a large bowl and add the spice mix. Mix it through with a spoon.

Heat some oil in a frying pan and add the chicken and vegetables. Stir-fry until the chicken is cooked through. You can check this by taking a piece out of the pan and cutting it in half. If it is completely white on the inside, it is cooked.

Place a spoonful of the chicken, peppers and onions in the middle of a tortilla wrap and add a little cheese, salsa and a dollop of sour cream. Finally, roll one side of the wrap over to the middle, then tuck in the end and roll the other side of the wrap over, then dig in.

CHILLI CON CARNE BURRITO

SERVES 4

2 tablespoons rapeseed oil

1 onion, chopped

Salt

1 clove of garlic, chopped

1 chilli (red or green), chopped

250g minced beef

1 teaspoon tomato purée

1 x 400g tin of tomatoes

1 teaspoon dried oregano

A few drops of Worcestershire sauce

100g long-grain rice, cooked according to instructions

Grated cheese

4 tortilla wraps (see p. 232)

Obviously you can just serve the chilli with rice but kids seem to love it even more as a burrito! How hot you make this is up to you – use less or more chilli to taste.

• • • • • • • • • • • •

To make the chilli sauce, heat the oil over a medium heat, then add the onion and a pinch of salt. Sweat the onion until it has softened, then add the garlic and chilli.

Add the mince and stir until the outside of the mince has browned, then add the tomato purée and stir to combine. Next, add the tinned tomatoes and, using the empty tin, add half a tin of water. Then sprinkle in the oregano and Worcestershire sauce.

Simmer gently for at least 30 minutes.

Place some of the rice and the chilli con carne into the middle of the wraps and top with the cheese. Roll one side over, tuck in the bottom and roll fully. If anyone finds this too hot, just add a dollop of sour cream to the wrap.

CHICKEN PARMIGIANA

SERVES 2

This started as a request from Katie, a regular attendee at our kids' camps, and turned out to be extremely popular with everyone. For a slightly more refined version, use buffalo mozzarella, sliced and placed on top of the chicken before placing under the grill.

• • • • • • • • • • • • •

1 portion tomato sauce (see p. 222)
50g plain flour
1 egg, lightly beaten
50g breadcrumbs
25g Parmesan, grated
25g mozzarella, grated
2 chicken fillets, skinned
Rapeseed/sunflower oil
Basil

First make the tomato sauce (see p. 222).

When the sauce is ready, place the flour, egg and breadcrumbs in separate shallow bowls. Mix half of the Parmesan and mozzarella together and place in another bowl. Dip the chicken into the flour and shake to remove any excess, then place into the egg, followed by the breadcrumbs and Parmesan mix.

In a shallow pan, heat a good glug of oil until very hot. Place the chicken onto the pan and fry on each side for about 3 minutes or until golden brown and cooked through.

Place the chicken in a dish and pour half the tomato sauce over each piece of chicken, then top with the remainder of the mozzarella and Parmesan mix and place under a hot grill to melt the cheese. Garnish with the basil and serve with spaghetti.

RASPBERRY CORDIAL

My daughter loves this raspberry cordial as a treat when she has friends over. We mix it with sparkling water or lemonade and serve it from a kilner dispenser. For the adults, as suggested by my friend Sinead, a little added to a glass of prosecco is a treat.

• ● • ● • ● • ● • ● • ● • ●

250g raspberries
Juice of ½ lemon
125g caster sugar
150ml water

Place the raspberries and a squeeze of lemon juice in a pot with the sugar. Cook gently over a low heat for 10 minutes, mashing every now and then.

Place a sieve over a clean pot and pour the mixture in. Add the water to the liquid in the pot and stir. Bring to the boil, then allow to cool. Store in sterilised bottles/jars until ready to use.

SNACKING ON THE COUCH

· · · · · · · · · · · · · · · · · · · ·

WORKING PHYSICALLY ALWAYS LEAVES ME TIRED AND I AM A DIVIL FOR HITTING THE COUCH WITH SNACKS. WITH THIS IN MIND, I DO TRY (NOT EVERY DAY MIND YOU) TO HAVE SNACKS THAT ARE A LITTLE BIT HEALTHIER THAN CRISPS. SNACKS WITHOUT THE GUILT!

HEALTHIER NACHOS WITH MANGO SALSA

SERVES 2-4

Everyone loves corn chips so why not try a less sinful version that is still totally delicious and satisfying? How many this serves depends on how greedy you are!

• • • • • • • • • • • • • •

2 corn tortillas

3 tablespoons olive oil

½ tablespoon freshly ground coriander (optional)

½ tablespoon freshly ground cumin (optional)

½ teaspoon salt

A large handful of grated cheese (strong cheddar is best)

FOR THE MANGO SALSA:

½ mango, peeled and chopped

½ red onion, finely chopped

1 red chilli, deseeded and finely chopped

Zest and juice from ½ lime

A small handful of coriander leaves

Salt

Preheat the oven to 220˚C/fan 200˚C/gas mark 7.

Combine all the ingredients for the salsa in a bowl. Add salt according to taste.

Cut the tortillas into eight wedges each, place in a big bowl and toss with the olive oil, spices (if using) and salt. Spread out flat on a baking tray and cook in the hot oven for about 3–4 minutes until slightly golden brown.

Remove from the oven and switch the grill on. Sprinkle the cheese over the nachos and place under the hot grill for a few minutes until the cheese has melted. Spoon the mango salsa over and enjoy.

BABA GHANOUSH

SERVES 4

Olive oil

2 aubergines

2 tablespoons tahini

Juice of ½ lemon

3 cloves of garlic

A bunch of flat-leaf parsley

Salt

Baba ghanoush and hummus are very similar in terms of the ingredients you use, except that here you are using roasted aubergine instead of chickpeas so they end up with a very different flavour and texture. Baba ghanoush has a lovely smokey flavour.

• • • • • • • • • • • •

Preheat the oven to 180°C/fan 160°C/gas mark 4.

Brush a baking tray lightly with olive oil. Slice the aubergines in half lengthways and place face down on the tray. Bake for about an hour or until soft.

When the aubergines are cool enough to handle, scoop out the flesh and place in a food processor with the tahini, lemon juice, garlic and parsley. Whizz for a few seconds and taste. Add salt to your taste.

This is lovely served with flatbreads or pittas, lightly oiled, seasoned with za'atar, baharat or harissa, and toasted.

HUMMUS

SERVES 4

I almost always have some hummus in the fridge, as it is a great, protein-packed snack, ideal for those days when you are hungry but have to wait for dinner! It's also a great after-school snack for kids. If you don't like this too spicy, then use less cayenne pepper. I often omit the garlic if I am sending this to school in my daughter's lunchbox.

• • • • • • • • • • • • •

1 x 400g tin of chickpeas

1 tablespoon tahini

2 cloves of garlic, chopped or minced

1 teaspoon cayenne pepper

Sea salt flakes

1 teaspoon lemon juice

3 tablespoons olive oil

In a food processor, or by hand, mash the chickpeas with the tahini, then add the garlic, cayenne and a generous pinch of salt.

Add the lemon juice, then drizzle in the olive oil, mixing, until the hummus is the consistency you require. You may need to add more oil to obtain this. You might also like to add more lemon juice, according to your taste. Taste and adjust the seasoning if necessary.

This is lovely served with flatbreads or pittas, lightly oiled, seasoned with za'atar, baharat or harissa, and toasted.

WHIPPED FETA

SERVES 4

I first started making this whipped feta a few Christmases ago. Anytime we had visitors during the festive period, I used them as an excuse to make a batch of this, when it was really me eating most of it!

100g feta cheese

100g mascarpone

Juice of ½ lemon

2 tablespoons olive oil

1 shallot (optional)

1 clove of garlic (optional)

Salt and pink peppercorns

Combine the feta, mascarpone, lemon juice, oil, shallot (if using) and garlic (if using) in a food processor and then season to taste. I love serving this with oat cakes.

• •

OLIVE TAPENADE

SERVES 4

This keeps for weeks in a sterilised jar in the fridge. It is delicious on top of crostini as a canapé.

110g black olives, stoned

50g anchovy fillets

1 tablespoon capers

1 teaspoon Dijon mustard

1 teaspoon freshly squeezed lemon juice

4 or 5 twists of black pepper

4 tablespoons olive oil

In a food processor, whiz up the olives with the anchovies, capers, mustard, lemon juice and pepper. Add the olive oil and blitz again to bind it. Serve with crudités or breadsticks.

FILO PARCELS

These little parcels of deliciousness are an ideal snack to have on the couch, but they are also a lovely canapé. So prepare a double quantity if you are making them for friends and stick half of them in the freezer for a lazy evening. These are a great snack, but served with some dressed green leaves also make a lovely light lunch or supper.

• • • • • • • • • • • •

MAKES 20

Rapeseed oil

1 onion, sliced and caramelised

1 roll of filo pastry

A knob of butter, melted

200g feta cheese, crumbled or chopped

A few olives (optional)

A handful of flat-leaf parsley, chopped

Juice of ½ lemon

Salt and pepper

1 tablespoon sesame seeds

Preheat the oven to 180°C/fan 160°C/gas mark 4.

Place a couple of tablespoons of oil in a frying pan over a medium heat, add the onion and cook until golden brown.

Carefully unwrap the filo pastry and lay out on a clean, lightly floured surface. Cut each sheet into three equal pieces and brush around the edges with the melted butter.

In the meantime, combine the onion, feta, olives, parsley and a good squeeze of lemon juice in a bowl and season with salt and pepper. Taste and adjust if necessary.

Carefully place a heaped teaspoon of the filling on one corner of a piece of filo pastry, avoiding the edges. Fold over neatly to create a triangle. Fold again, working all the way up until you have a neat triangle.

Brush with more butter and sprinkle with sesame seeds. Place on a baking tray and bake for 15–20 minutes or until golden and crisp.

TARA'S TIP:

ONE TIP I ALWAYS GIVE AT MY COOKERY CLASSES IS TO ADD A PINCH OF SALT TO ONION AND GARLIC TO SLOW DOWN THE CARAMELISATION PROCESS AND GIVE DEPTH OF FLAVOUR.

DESSERTS + BAKING

· ·

I FIND MANY PEOPLE WHO ATTEND MY CLASSES ARE EITHER REALLY
INTO BAKING OR AREN'T AT ALL, WITH NO MIDDLE GROUND. I WOULD
FALL INTO THE LATTER CATEGORY IN MY DAY-TO-DAY LIFE, BUT I DO
LOVE TO HAVE A NICE DESSERT AFTER A SPECIAL MEAL OR ON A
SUNDAY AFTER THE ROAST. I HAVE PROVIDED A COUPLE OF MASTER
RECIPES HERE, FOR CHEESECAKE AND CUPCAKES, AS I FIND IT VERY
HANDY TO HAVE A BASE RECIPE THAT I CAN FLAVOUR WITH WHATEVER
FRESH/FROZEN/DRIED FRUIT OR CHOCOLATE I HAVE AROUND THE
HOUSE, OR SPICES SUCH AS CINNAMON AND VANILLA IF I'M LOW
ON OTHER INGREDIENTS. I SOMETIMES MAKE THE CUPCAKE MASTER
RECIPE AS MINI LOAVES AND JUST DRIZZLE SOME MELTED CHOCOLATE
OVER THEM AS I'M NOT A BIG FAN OF BUTTERCREAM (ALTHOUGH
ALMOST ALL CHILDREN SEEM TO LOVE IT!).

STRAWBERRIES WITH BASIL, BALSAMIC, MASCARPONE + HAZELNUT SABLES

SERVES 6–8

This is a take on a recipe I learned at Le Cordon Bleu in Paris, but once you have made the shortbread most of the work is done. This recipe may seem like an odd combination at first, but it is really fresh and light – perfect for *al fresco* entertaining. There are a few steps in it but they are all easy and the whole thing should take no longer than about 30 minutes. Go ahead – try it, you'll love it!

• • • • • • • • • • • • • •

125g plain flour

30g icing sugar

Salt

85g butter, cold and cut into squares

30g whole hazelnuts, roughly chopped (do not use shop-bought chopped hazelnuts)

200ml freshly squeezed orange juice

50g caster sugar

4 stalks of basil, leaves and stalks separated

50ml balsamic vinegar

1 punnet of strawberries, sliced and stalks removed

Olive oil

150g mascarpone

1 teaspoon vanilla extract

100ml cream, whipped

Preheat the oven to 180°C/fan 160°C/gas mark 4.

Sieve the flour into a bowl and add the icing sugar and a pinch of salt. Rub the butter into the mixture with your fingertips until it resembles breadcrumbs. Turn out on to a floured surface and knead the dough for a couple of minutes. Don't overknead, as it will lose its lovely light texture. Leave to rest for 10 minutes.

Roll out the dough to half a centimetre thickness (it should not be sticky so you will not need to flour the surface). Cut out the biscuit shape you want – I recommend fingers as they can be used to scoop up the mascarpone later.

Push the hazelnuts into the dough, then bake for 8–12 minutes on a baking tray.

While the sables are cooking, place the orange juice in a pot with most of the caster sugar (keeping 1 tablespoon back) and a few basil stalks. Warm very gently to allow the flavours to infuse – it is important not to overheat this or the flavours will be spoiled. Leave to cool.

In a separate pot, reduce the balsamic vinegar until it becomes a syrup.

Place the strawberries in a bowl, add the tablespoon of sugar, a pinch of salt and the balsamic vinegar reduction. Allow to macerate for at least 10 minutes, if not more.

Place a little olive oil in a pot and add the basil leaves and a small pinch of salt. Warm gently and break down with the back of a spoon, stirring until you have a rough paste.

Place the mascarpone in a bowl and whisk a little to loosen. Add the basil paste and vanilla extract. Fold in the whipped cream.

To serve, place two sables on a plate, and top with some of the strawberries and a dollop of the mascarpone mix. Strain the orange-juice sauce mixture into a jug or bowl, then drizzle a little over the mascarpone mix. Finally spoon a little of the balsamic and strawberry juice around the edge of the plate.

PAULA'S PUMPKIN PIE

MAKES 1 PIE

The filling can be made easy if you use canned pumpkin purée, but it can be hard to find.

• • • • • • • • • • • • •

FOR THE PASTRY:

250g plain flour

1 teaspoon salt

1 teaspoon sugar

230g unsalted butter, chilled and cut into small pieces

60–120ml iced water

FOR THE PIE FILLING:

1 large pumpkin

2 eggs

235g fresh cream

165g muscovado sugar

1 teaspoon cinnamon

½ teaspoon orange zest

½ teaspoon salt

½ teaspoon allspice

½ teaspoon ground cloves

½ teaspoon ground ginger

½ teaspoon nutmeg

FOR THE CHANTILLY CREAM:

235ml fresh cream

2–3 tablespoons icing sugar

½ teaspoon vanilla extract, vanilla powder or vanilla paste

Cut the pumpkin in half and clean out the seeds. Cut into small pieces, place on a baking sheet and bake in the oven at 180˚C/fan 160˚C/gas mark 4 for 30–45 minutes, or until soft. Let it cool, then remove the flesh from the skin and purée or mash it with the back of a fork. Leave the pulp in a fine-meshed sieve over a bowl for at least 2 hours, or overnight if possible, to allow excess water to drain out.

Make the pastry. In a bowl, combine the flour, salt and sugar. Add the butter and quickly crumble this into the flour with your fingertips until the mixture resembles coarse breadcrumbs. Stir in the water, a tablespoon at a time, until the mixture forms a firm ball. Divide in two and wrap in cling film. Freeze one portion and refrigerate the other for at least 1 hour or, if possible, overnight.

Preheat the oven to 230°C/fan 210°C /gas mark 8.

Roll out the pastry and place in a 9-inch pie dish. Crimp the edges between your fingers.

Mix 400g pumpkin together with the rest of the ingredients for the pie filling and pour into the pastry. Bake for 15 minutes, then reduce the heat to 180°C/fan 160°C/gas mark 4 for 25 more minutes, or until the tip of a sharp knife inserted comes out clean. Let cool for at least 10 minutes before serving.

To make the Chantilly cream, whisk the cream, sugar and vanilla in a large bowl until soft peaks form. The cream should hold its shape but still be satiny in appearance.

Once cool, slice the pie and serve with the Chantilly whipped cream.

LEMON THUMBPRINT GEMS

MAKES 12

Once you have mastered the shortbread recipe, you can choose to make or buy the lemon curd for this simple but delicious afternoon treat or dessert. Substitute one large orange for the lemon to turn it into orange curd.

• • • • • • • • • • • •

125g butter, softened

30g caster sugar

½ egg yolk

Juice and zest of ½ lemon

125g plain flour

25g ground almonds

10g cornflour

FOR THE LEMON CURD:

1 egg

1 egg yolk

50g butter

90g caster sugar

Zest (finely grated) and juice of 2 lemons

Preheat the oven to 180˚C/fan 160˚C /gas mark 4. Line two baking sheets with greaseproof paper.

To make the dough, beat together the butter and sugar. Add the egg yolk, lemon zest and juice. You can use an electric mixer here, but we aren't really creaming so it is not necessary.

Fold in the flour, ground almonds and cornflour. Do this gently – it should be just combined. The dough is very sticky so it goes in the fridge to chill for an hour.

Remove the dough from the fridge and roll into cherry tomato-sized balls. Space these evenly on your baking sheets. Make an indentation in the centre of each biscuit by pressing down with your thumb and wiggling it about to make it slightly bigger than your thumb. The indentation needs to be able to hold half a teaspoon of the lemon curd. Bake for 20–25 minutes until golden.

While waiting for the gems to cook, make the lemon curd. In a bowl, whisk together the egg and the egg yolk. Melt the butter in a saucepan over a very low heat. Add the caster sugar, lemon zest and juice, and then the beaten eggs. Stir carefully with a wooden spoon, over a very gentle heat until the mixture thickens. This should take about 7–10 minutes. If the heat is too high, the egg will scramble. The curd is ready when the mixture is thick enough to coat the back of the wooden spoon and show a definite mark when you push your finger through it.

Remove from the heat and allow to cool.

The moment the biscuits come out of the oven, fill each indentation with half a teaspoon of lemon curd. Then transfer them from the baking sheet to wire racks to cool.

CHOCOLATE + ORANGE 'WEB' CAKE

MAKES 1 CAKE

This is the easiest cake ever. You basically put everything in a bowl and mix. I serve it with cream-cheese frosting in the centre and melted chocolate on top, but feel free just to do some buttercream or chocolate sauce with it. It will still be delicious. It's an ideal birthday cake too.

• • • • • • • • • • • • •

175g self-raising flour

1 rounded teaspoon baking powder

50g cocoa powder

3 eggs

4 tablespoons milk

100ml sunflower oil

250g caster sugar

½ teaspoon orange blossom water

90ml boiling water

FOR THE FROSTING:

100g cream cheese

50g butter

1 teaspoon vanilla extract

1 orange, zested and juiced

65g icing sugar

FOR THE CHOCOLATE DECORATION:

100g dark chocolate

15g white chocolate

Preheat the oven to 180°C/fan 160°C/gas mark 4 and line a 9-inch cake tin.

Sieve the flour and baking powder into a large mixing bowl, then add the rest of the cake ingredients, except for the boiling water. Using a wooden spoon or electric whisk, beat the mixture until smooth and well combined.

Add the boiling water to the mixture, a little at a time, until the consistency is smooth. (The cake mixture will now be very liquid.) Pour the cake mixture into the cake tin and bake for about 20–25 minutes.

While the cake is cooking, make the frosting. Beat the cream cheese and butter until soft and smooth. Add in the vanilla extract and a tablespoon of the orange juice and all the zest, then sieve in the sugar and beat for a few moments until the mixture is completely smooth.

Remove the cake from the oven and allow to cool. When totally cool, cut it in half widthways. Spread the frosting on one half of the cake, then place the second half of the cake on top.

Melt the dark chocolate and pour it over the cake evenly. Allow to cool for a couple of minutes.

In the meantime, melt the white chocolate and place in a piping bag with a very small hole (or use a small freezer bag and cut the hole in the corner).

When the dark chocolate is cool, draw a large circle around the perimeter of the cake with the white chocolate, then another smaller circle about a centimetre in and another, and so on, until you reach the centre. Place a sharp point such as a skewer or knife in the centre of the cake and pull it through the white chocolate until you reach the edge, creating a spiderweb effect. Repeat at regular intervals.

TARA'S TIP:

IF YOU CAN'T FIND ORANGE BLOSSOM WATER YOU CAN USE FRESHLY SQUEEZED ORANGE JUICE.

SONIA'S TRADITIONAL COZONAC

SERVES 8

Sonia works at the cookery school with me and brought us this recipe a few years ago. It is traditionally eaten at Christmas time in her home in Transylvania. We made it at the kids' camp and the kids absolutely loved it.

• • • • • • • • • • • •

250g plain flour

50ml milk

½ sachet (7g) of dried yeast

1 egg

1 egg yolk

25g sugar

½ teaspoon vanilla extract

25g butter, melted

Zest of ½ lemon

FOR THE FILLING:

1 egg white

75g ground walnuts

35g sugar

½ tablespoon cocoa

Put the flour into a large bowl and make a little well in the middle. Heat the milk until it is lukewarm, then mix in the yeast and pour into the well.

Add the egg, egg yolk (saving a teaspoonful for later), sugar, vanilla extract, butter and lemon zest. Mix well and knead for at least 15 minutes, adding an extra bit of lukewarm water if it gets dry, or extra flour if it's too wet, until the dough separates from the bowl. Let the dough rest for at least 20 minutes.

Preheat the oven to 180°C/fan 160°C/gas mark 4.

To make the filling, whisk the egg white until stiff, then mix in the walnuts, sugar and cocoa.

Separate the dough into two equal parts and roll each into a rectangular shape about 25 x 35cm. Spread half the walnut mix over one rectangle, then gently roll it up. Repeat with the rest of the filling and the second rectangle.

Let the rolls rest for 10 minutes, then brush with the leftover egg yolk and bake for about 45–50 minutes. When baked they will be a lovely golden brown. Allow to cool to room temperature, then slice and enjoy.

BANANA + APRICOT FLAPJACKS WITH CHOCOLATE SWIRL TOPPING

MAKES 9

Kids love this recipe and these flapjacks are great for lunchboxes. Make a batch and they should keep you going for a few days as a not-too-naughty treat.

• • • • • • • • • • • • • • •

150g butter

150ml golden syrup

375g porridge oats

55g dried apricots (or any dried fruit you fancy), chopped

2 large bananas, well mashed

100g milk chocolate

15g white chocolate

Preheat the oven to 190°C/170°C fan/gas mark 5.

Melt the butter in a jug or pot and add the golden syrup, mixing well.

Put the oats in a large mixing bowl, then add the butter/syrup mix, the apricots and mashed banana and stir well until all the oats have been coated in the buttery mixture.

Transfer the mixture to an 8 x 8-inch baking tray lined with greaseproof paper and level the surface. Bake in the oven for 10 minutes until the top is just beginning to turn a pale golden colour. The mixture will still seem somewhat soft. Allow to cool in the tin before decorating.

Once the flapjacks have cooled, melt the milk chocolate and pour it over them evenly. Allow the chocolate to cool for a couple of minutes. In the meantime, melt the white chocolate and place it in a piping bag with a very small hole. Use the piping bag to draw 'lines' of white chocolate on top of the milk chocolate from top to bottom at regular intervals.

Using a sharp point, such as a skewer or knife, draw it from side to side through the white chocolate in evenly spaced intervals to create a nice pattern.

When the chocolate has set you can slice the flapjacks.

TARA'S TIP:

YOU CAN USE A FORK TO DRIZZLE THE WHITE CHOCOLATE IF YOU CAN'T BE BOTHERED WITH A PIPING BAG.

SALTED CARAMEL MINI BANOFFEE PIES

MAKES 6

100g digestive biscuits

75g butter, melted

3 bananas, sliced

100ml cream, softly whipped

A couple of squares of chocolate for grating

FOR THE SALTED CARAMEL:

225g sugar, caster or granulated

75ml water

110g butter

175ml regular or double cream

Sea salt flakes

This recipe is the reason I make salted caramel. These mini pies are nothing like the stodgy banoffees that many people expect, as they are very light.

• • • • • • • • • • • • • •

First make the caramel. Place the sugar and the water in a saucepan over a medium heat and stir as it heats up to dissolve the sugar.

Once the sugar has dissolved, stir in the butter, turn the heat up to high and cook for about 10 minutes until it turns a toffee colour. Do not stir at this stage, though you might need to swirl the pan occasionally if you see it turning golden on one side of the pan before the other.

Once it is a rich golden toffee colour, take it off the heat for a moment, then stir in half the cream. When the bubbles die down, stir in the rest of the cream and a pinch of salt to taste (how much you use depends on your taste preference).

Bash up the biscuits in a bowl or food processor or freezer bag. Add the melted butter and mix. Place even amounts of the biscuit mixture in the bottom of six mini tartlet tins (these are also lovely served in vintage-style cups), flatten and top with the sliced bananas. Pour equal amounts of the salted caramel over each and leave to set in the fridge for at least 30 minutes. Top with the softly whipped cream and decorate with some grated chocolate.

SPICED ROASTED PINEAPPLE WITH SAFFRON + CARDAMOM CUSTARD + CANDIED PISTACHIOS

SERVES 4

This is a gorgeous and easy recipe. Don't be put off by the long list of ingredients as you should have most of these in your store cupboard. This is the very popular dessert from our Indian class.

• • • • • • • • • • • • • •

A large handful of unsalted pistachio nuts

200g caster sugar, plus extra for candying the pistachios

4 green cardamom pods, lightly crushed

A small pinch of saffron strands

3 star anise

1 cinnamon stick, broken

8 black peppercorns, whole

10 fennel seeds

300ml water

1 ripe pineapple, peeled, core removed, chopped into 8 equal-sized pieces

FOR THE CUSTARD:

4 egg yolks

60g caster sugar

250ml single cream

A large pinch of saffron threads (about 1 teaspoon)

7–8 cardamom pods

Preheat the oven to 180°C/fan 160°C/gas mark 4.

Toast the pistachios on a dry pan and then chop. Candy the nuts by wetting them with a few drops of water and tossing them in two teaspoons of caster sugar. Place on a baking tray lined with greaseproof paper and put in the oven for 5–10 minutes – they are ready when they turn golden. Remove from the oven and allow to cool. When they have cooled, bash them a little to break them up.

Increase the heat of the oven to 200°C /fan 180°C/gas mark 6.

Place the sugar and spices into a heavy-based pan and pour over the water. Bring the mixture to the boil, stirring well so that the sugar dissolves, then reduce the heat until the mixture is simmering and continue to simmer for 8–10 minutes, or until the mixture has thickened and resembles syrup. Strain the mixture into a clean jug, discarding the whole spices.

Lay the pineapple pieces onto a roasting tray. Drizzle over two-thirds of the sugar syrup, then transfer to the oven and roast for 8–10 minutes, basting regularly with the remaining sugar syrup.

While the pineapple is cooking, make the custard. Place the egg yolks and sugar in a bowl and whisk until the sugar has dissolved into the eggs and the mixture becomes pale in colour. Set aside.

Place the cream in a saucepan with the saffron and cardamom pods and heat very gently until it just about reaches boiling point. You will be able to see the surface quivering. Turn the heat off and allow the cream to infuse with the saffron and cardamom for 3–4 minutes.

Place a strainer over a jug and pour the cream in, removing the saffron and cardamom.

Pour a small amount of the flavoured cream into the egg mixture and whisk (this is to temper the eggs). Then pour the egg mixture into the saucepan along with the rest of the cream. Over a gentle heat, stir the custard until it thickens. When it is thick enough to coat the back of a spoon, remove from the heat and return to the jug.

To serve, arrange two pieces of spiced, roasted pineapple in the centre of four serving plates. Top with some of the custard and a few candied pistachios.

SALTED CARAMEL MILLIONAIRE'S SHORTBREAD

MAKES 9

125g plain flour

30g icing sugar

A pinch of salt

85g butter, cold and cut into squares

1 portion of salted caramel (see p. 263)

180g dark (50% or 60% cocoa solids) or milk chocolate

Another great way to justify making a salted caramel!

• • • • • • • • • • • •

Preheat the oven to 180°C/fan 160°C/gas mark 4.

Sieve the flour into a bowl and add the icing sugar and salt.

Rub the butter into the mixture with your fingertips until it resembles breadcrumbs. Put this mixture on your work surface and use your hands to bring it all together into a dough.

Knead the dough on a floured surface for a couple of minutes and leave to rest for 10 minutes.

Line an 8 x 8-inch baking tray with greaseproof paper. Roll out the dough to the size of the tin – it should not be sticky so you will not need to flour the surface. Place the dough into the baking tin, and if necessary use your fingers to push it out so it completely fills the tin. Bake for 8–12 minutes, then remove from the oven and allow to cool.

Make the salted caramel (see p. 263). Once the shortbread base is cool, pour the caramel onto it and place in the fridge for at least 30 minutes to set.

When the caramel is set, melt the chocolate and pour evenly over the caramel. Allow the chocolate to set before cutting.

LIZ'S CHERRY, CHOCOLATE + ALMOND CAKE

MAKES 1 CAKE

My friend Liz once served me this cake with a cup of coffee and I never forgot it. I'm not a mad cake eater but this one is absolutely delicious and well worth making if you have visitors coming! The cherries are a little boring to prepare, but the rest is very quick and easy to do.

• • • • • • • • • • • • • • •

200g butter

200g soft light-brown sugar

3 eggs

2 tablespoons milk

1 teaspoon almond extract

150g self-raising flour

50g ground almonds

100g milk chocolate, chips or chopped

150g fresh cherries, halved and pitted

FOR THE TOPPING:

50g milk chocolate

50g toasted flaked almonds

Preheat the oven to 180°C/fan 160°C/gas mark 4. Line a 9-inch tin with greaseproof paper (I always use a springform cake tin to make it easy to get out).

Make sure the butter is fairly soft – put into the microwave for 20 seconds if necessary. Cream the butter and sugar together well, using an electric whisk or mixer if possible.

Add the eggs in, one by one, mixing between each one. Don't worry if it looks curdled, the flour will rectify this. Add the milk and almond extract and mix well.

Fold in the flour, ground almonds, chocolate and cherries (keeping a few back to decorate), and place in the oven for about 45 minutes or until cooked through. When it is cooked, a skewer inserted in the middle should come out clean and dry. If the cake starts to brown too much within the first 30 minutes of baking, place a sheet of tinfoil over the top, loosely securing the sides.

Allow to cool before removing from the tin.

Melt the chocolate and drizzle over the cake, then top with the remaining cherries and the flaked almonds.

CHEESECAKE 3 WAYS

SERVES 12

Although most recipe books will give you various cheesecake recipes, I prefer to let people make up their own mind on flavours. So what I have provided here is a master recipe, to which you can add the flavours your prefer. I find cheesecake a very handy dessert if you have guests over as you can make it earlier in the day and it really doesn't need to be served with anything on the side. All you have to do is slice it and put it on a plate. This recipe can also be used for individual cheesecakes served in little cups and saucers.

• • • • • • • • • • •

250g digestive biscuits

125g butter

450g cream cheese

225g caster sugar

400g double cream

1 teaspoon pure vanilla extract

Place the biscuits in a large bowl and crush with a rolling pin. Melt the butter, then mix through the biscuit crumbs. Line a 10-inch cake tin with cling film, then spoon in the biscuit mixture and flatten as evenly as you can. Refrigerate for a minimum of 2 hours.

Mix the cream cheese, caster sugar and cream in a bowl until you have a stiff mixture. This should take 3–4 minutes. Add the vanilla extract at the end.

Spread the cheese mixture on the biscuit base and refrigerate until set, then remove carefully from the tin.

SUGGESTED CHEESECAKE FLAVOURINGS
BERRY RIPPLE: Make the mixed-berry compote on page 38. Cool a little and then drizzle in concentric circles over the set cheesecake. Using a skewer, make a ripple effect across the surface. Top with fresh berries.

BAILEY'S: Add 30ml Baileys to the bowl along with the other ingredients. To decorate, grate 25g dark chocolate and sprinkle over the set cheesecake.

LEMON: Add most of the zest of 1 lemon (keeping a little back to decorate) and the juice of 1–2 lemons (about 4 tablespoons) to the bowl along with all the other ingredients.

MERINGUE SWIRLS WITH LEMON CURD + CREAM

MAKES 6

Who doesn't love a meringue? Lemon and meringue is a classic combo. These swirls are great to prepare ahead of time and just assemble if you have guests coming.

• • • • • • • • • • • • • •

2 egg whites

A pinch of salt

150g caster sugar

¼ teaspoon vanilla extract

Red food colouring

Lemon curd (see p. 254)

250ml cream, whipped

Preheat the oven to 140°C/fan 120°C/gas mark 1 and line a 10 x 14-inch baking tray with baking paper.

Put the egg whites into a large spotlessly clean mixing bowl with the salt. Whisk until soft peaks form, then gradually add the caster sugar, continuing to whip, until stiff peaks form. Fold in the vanilla extract.

Place the food colouring in the bowl and use a skewer to swirl the colouring into the meringues to give a ripple effect.

Using a large spoon dollop the meringues onto the baking sheet, leaving plenty of space between them.

Bake for 30 minutes or until the base of the meringues is hard and then switch off the oven. Leave to cool in the oven if possible.

While waiting for the meringues to cool, make the lemon curd (see p. 254).

To serve, gently mix the whipped cream with the lemon curd and spoon onto the meringues.

GLUTEN-FREE MINI LEMON + MINT POLENTA CAKES

MAKES APPROX. 10,
DEPENDING ON THE SIZE OF YOUR CAKE
PAPERS/LOAF BOXES

230g butter

230g caster sugar

4 large eggs

140g polenta

200g ground almonds

2 teaspoons baking powder
(make sure it is gluten-free)

Zest and juice 1 lemon

A couple of sprigs of mint, chopped

100g icing sugar

This recipe can also be used for a full cake in a 9-inch tin.
Bake for an hour if doing a whole cake.

• • • • • • • • • • • •

Preheat the oven to 160°C/fan 140°C/gas mark 3. Line
up about ten mini cake papers or loaf boxes on a baking
tray.

Cream the butter and sugar together until light and
fluffy. Add the eggs one at a time and mix thoroughly.
Once the mixture is combined, add the polenta, ground
almonds, baking powder, lemon zest and juice (saving
3 tablespoons for the icing), and the mint.

Transfer the mixture to the cake papers or loaf boxes,
spread evenly, then cook for about 30 minutes or until
a skewer inserted into the centre of the cake comes out
clean. Let the cakes cool to room temperature.

Mix the icing sugar with 3 tablespoons of lemon juice
until the lumps have disappeared. Drizzle the lemon
glaze over the top of the cakes when they are cool and
garnish with some mint flowers or leaves.

TARA'S TIP:

FOR A GORGEOUS TWO-TONE EFFECT IN CUPCAKE
ICING, TAKE HALF THE BUTTERCREAM OUT OF THE MIXER
BEFORE YOU FLAVOUR OR COLOUR IT AND PLACE IT IN
A PIPING BAG, KEEPING IT TO ONE SIDE. COLOUR AND
FLAVOUR THE REST OF THE BUTTERCREAM AND ADD
IT TO THE OTHER SIDE OF THE BAG. WHEN YOU START
PIPING, IT SHOULD COME OUT TWO-TONE. TO MAKE
FILLING YOUR PIPING BAG EASIER, PUT IT IN A TALL,
THIN JUG OR PINT GLASS AND FOLD THE EDGE
OVER TO HOLD IT IN PLACE WHILE
YOU FILL IT.

CUPCAKES LOTS OF WAYS

You can use the basic recipe here and add any type of flavour extract you wish, such as vanilla, lemon, strawberry or almond, as well as any food colouring, to create whatever flavours you want. You can leave these with just the buttercream topping, but if you want to go all out, you can add sprinkles, marshmallows, chopped dark or white chocolate, raspberries or blueberries, or chopped mixed dried fruit and cinnamon.

• • • • • • • • • • • • •

MAKES 12

110g butter, softened

110g caster sugar

½ teaspoon vanilla extract

2 eggs

50ml milk

175g plain flour

1 teaspoon baking powder

FOR THE BUTTERCREAM ICING:

150g butter, softened

150g icing sugar

A few drops of your chosen extract, e.g. vanilla, lemon, strawberry or almond

A few drops of food colouring of your choice

SUGGESTED CUPCAKE FILLINGS:

55g dark chocolate, chopped and 1 large banana, mashed

55g white chocolate, chopped, and raspberries or blueberries

30g dried mixed fruit and 1 teaspoon cinnamon

Preheat the oven to 190°C/fan 170°C/gas mark 5. Line a 12-hole muffin tray with muffin cases.

With a whisk, beat the butter, sugar and vanilla extract together until light and fluffy. Add the eggs one by one, mixing in between each, and then the milk. Add the flour and baking powder and mix until just combined.

Place a tablespoon of the batter into each paper case, add your chosen filling (see suggestions in ingredients list) and top with a teaspoon of the batter.

Bake for 15–20 minutes until golden brown and firm on the top. Remove from the oven and allow to cool.

To make the buttercream, whisk the butter until light and fluffy, then add the icing sugar. Stir in a few drops of your chosen flavour essence and food colouring.

When the cupcakes are completely cool, use a piping bag to top with the buttercream icing in a swirl.

BILLIE'S CHOCOLATE, AMARETTI + ORANGE CAKE

SERVES 12

When I first started teaching cookery years ago with Billie O'Shea at Fairyhouse Cookery School, I fell in love with this cake. It is dense, squidgy and absolutely delicious. I always say it has a great return on investment, as it is so quick and easy to make but is an impressive dessert. It's almost nicer the next day with a cup of coffee!

• • • • • • • • • • • • •

150g dark chocolate, broken into pieces

100g butter, cubed

50g Amaretti biscuits

100g ground almonds

175g sugar

4 eggs

Zest of 1 orange

FOR THE ICING (OPTIONAL):

2–3 teaspoons strong espresso powder

1 x 250g tub of mascarpone

A little orange zest

50g icing sugar, sieved

Preheat the oven to 180°C/fan 160°C/gas mark 4.

Grease an 8-inch springform cake tin and line the base with greaseproof paper.

Break the chocolate in a bowl and add the butter. Stand the bowl over a saucepan of just-simmering water until the chocolate and butter have melted (or melt in the microwave for a minute on high). Mix together and allow to cool slightly.

Bash the biscuits in a bowl with a rolling pin, then add the ground almonds, sugar and eggs and combine with a whisk. Add the melted chocolate and orange zest to the mixture and mix well.

Pour the batter into the cake tin and bake for about 35 minutes. When ready, the cake will have risen and started to crack at the top and the edges will be coming away from the side of the tin slightly.

Leave to cool for 5 minutes, then run a knife round to separate the cake from the tin and release the clip. Once cold transfer it to a plate. The cake can be served as it is in small slices, but it is lovely topped with a mascarpone coffee-cream icing.

To make the icing dissolve the espresso powder in
3 tablespoons of boiling water. Mix the mascarpone
and orange zest in a bowl, then slowly work in the icing
sugar, a third at a time, until you have a thick paste (an
electric beater is great for this). Finally beat in the coffee
paste, a spoonful at a time. Smooth the mascarpone
icing over the cake with a palette knife when cool and
serve.

INDEX

MERCIER PRESS

Cork

www.mercierpress.ie

© Tara Walker, 2017

www.eastcoastcookeryschool.ie

Photographed by Rob Kerkvliet – www.afoxinthekitchen.com

Styled by Jette Virdi – www.jettevirdi.com

Props from Created+Found homeware

Images on pages 5–10 and 288 courtesy of Sarah O'Flaherty

ISBN: 978 1 78117 477 7

10 9 8 7 6 5 4 3 2 1

A CIP record for this title is available from the British Library

Printed and bound in the EU.